DISCOVER**POOLE**

DISCOVER**POOLE**

AND THE MAIN PLACES OF INTEREST IN THE ISLE OF PURBECK, WAREHAM & WIMBORNE MINSTER

To Rosemary with much love Rod

RODNEY COOPER

Rodney F Cooper

22/8/11

HALSGROVE

First published in Great Britain in 2011

British Library Cataloguing-in-Publication Data
A CIP record for this title is available from the British Library

ISBN 978 0 85704 091 6

HALSGROVE
Halsgrove House,
Ryelands Industrial Park,
Bagley Road, Wellington, Somerset TA21 9PZ
Tel: 01823 653777   Fax: 01823 216796
email: sales@halsgrove.com

Part of the Halsgrove group of companies
Information on all Halsgrove titles is available at: www.halsgrove.com

Printed and bound in China by Everbest Printing Co Ltd

CONTENTS

INTRODUCTION

Discover Poole is a companion volume to *Discover Bournemouth* and follows a similar format. Whilst Bournemouth is a relatively modern town with a history dating back only 200 years, the history of Poole dates from much early times, as do all of the villages mentioned in this book.

Poole itself has many interesting ancient buildings on and around the quay and villas built at the height of the town's wealth. From the quay, boats leave to Brownsea Island, Wareham and along the Purbeck coast to the World Heritage Site of the Jurassic Coast. Poole's beaches are amongst the best in the country, whilst the shallow harbour is ideal for water sports.

The chain ferry from the Haven Hotel offers an interesting introduction to the Isle of Purbeck where there are excellent country, cliff and beach walks suitable for both beginners and experienced walkers. The old villages of Langton Matravers, Worth Matravers and Kingston retain much of the charm of past eras, as does the ghost village of Tyneham. Not to be missed is a visit to the village of Corfe Castle – its castle was one of the finest in England until blown up by the Parliamentarians during the Civil War and now offers an imposing ruin.

Wareham with the remains of its earth walls and its Saxon church is fascinating and well worth a visit. Lawrence of Arabia's connection to the town is much in evidence and a trip to the area would not be complete without a visit to Clouds Hill Cottage, the beautiful church at Moreton and the world famous Tank Museum at Bovington.

To the north of the Purbeck Peninsula is the town of Wimborne Minster with its historical church. Nearby is Kingston Lacy House with its outstanding collection of paintings and beautiful grounds.

The entire area is fascinating with beautiful countryside, charming villages and old churches.

Directions to the locations are generally from Bournemouth since it is here that most visitors to the area will stay due to its large number of hotels.

Acknowledgements

I would like to thank the many people I have spoken with, whose comments have aided me in writing the text. Above all thanks to my wife, Elaine, who somehow has stayed with me for forty years whilst I have been engaged in time consuming projects such as writing this book!

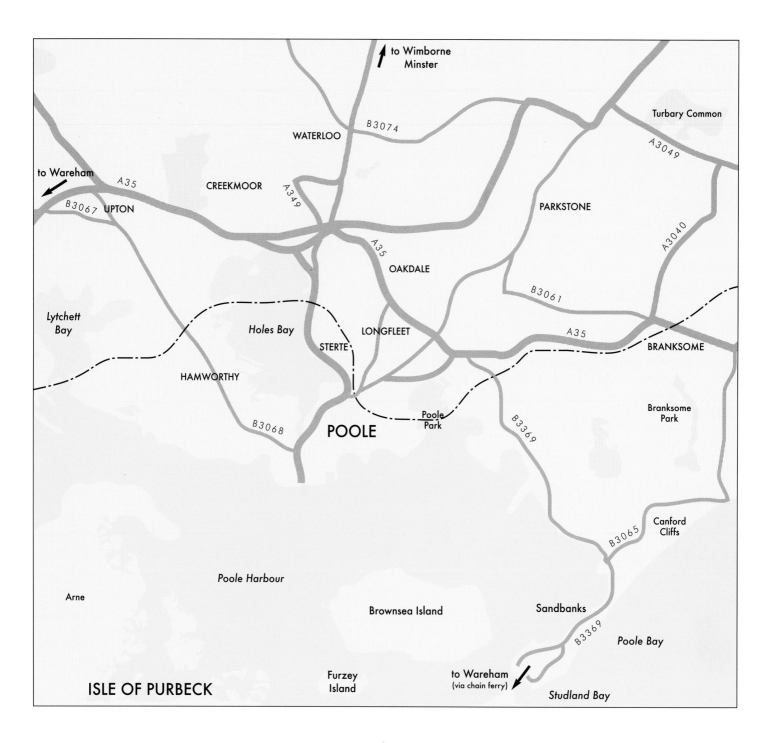

to Wimborne Minster

Turbary Common

WATERLOO

B3074

A3049

to Wareham

A35

CREEKMOOR

A349

PARKSTONE

B3067   UPTON

A35

A3040

OAKDALE

B3061

Lytchett Bay

Holes Bay

A35

BRANKSOME

LONGFLEET

STERTE

HAMWORTHY

Branksome Park

B3068

Poole Park

POOLE

B3369

Canford Cliffs

B3065

Poole Harbour

Arne

Brownsea Island

Sandbanks

Furzey Island

B3369

Poole Bay

ISLE OF PURBECK

to Wareham (via chain ferry)

Studland Bay

POOLE

The logboat, now in the **Poole Museum**, indicates that trade was taking place between Poole and the continent of Europe as early as 300BC when at that time the local Iron Age tribes lived around Wareham. The Roman Emperor, Vespasian, landed in Poole with his legion in 43 AD in his conquest of Britain and established the port of Hamworthy. The Romans continued to use the harbour for as along as they occupied the country. Wareham was a stronghold of the Saxons in the seventh century following their invasion of the country. The Vikings captured Wareham in 876 AD but were later defeated by the Saxon army and a violent storm destroyed most of their ships as they were escaping from Poole Harbour. Cnut landed in Poole from Norway in 1015, rapidly seized control of Wessex and declared himself King He remained one of the most powerful monarchs in Europe until his death in 1035.

Poole remained a small fishing town until the Norman rule during which period in 1248 the Charter of Liberties was sold to Poole, allowing Poole to appoint a mayor, hold a court in the town and gain exemption from other tolls and customs duties. With the silting up of the River Frome seamen and traders moved from Wareham to Poole. By the fifteenth century it was the biggest port in Dorset, mainly for wool exports with links from the Baltics to Italy. At this time Poole achieved Port of Staple status which meant that it now had a licence to build fortifications and in 1568 Poole was made a county by Queen Elizabeth I, which it remained until the eighteenth century.

An already established trade with North America increased during the seventeenth century, This trade with Newfoundland brought great wealth to Poole which became one of the principal British trading ports with North America. During the late eighteenth and early nineteenth centuries much of the development of the Old Town took place with the building of magnificent Georgian mansions (see for example Beech House - page 18). At the beginning of the nineteenth century, 90% of the population was employed on the harbour. Poole continued to flourish, growing ever more prosperous based largely on its fishing fleet which fished for cod in Newfoundland. The Poole ships took essential clothes and food to Newfoundland and then the salted fish, either to the West Indies to feed the slaves and then return to Poole with rum and molasses, or to Portugal, Spain and Italy and then returning to Poole with cargos of wine and fruit.

There was a rapid change of fortune with the end of the Napoleonic wars when the French were able to carry out the trade more cheaply and Britain lost its monopoly. Added to this was the fact that the invention of the railway meant that goods could be more cheaply carried by rail than by sea and that deeper hulled boats could use Southampton, which is nearer to London. During the 1940s the harbour was the base for flying boats and, together with Hurn Airport, is considered by many to be the birthplace of British Overseas Airways Corporation (BOAC), now known as BA. Today, although Poole still has a small fishing fleet, the harbour is mainly used by pleasure craft and only a small percentage of the population is directly employed on the harbour.

BOURNEMOUTH TO POOLE

Visitors leaving Bournemouth on the A338 Wessex Way come to the Boundary Roundabout, just after passing the 'Welcome to Poole' sign. Directly across (3rd exit) is The Avenue, leading to the Poole Beaches (page 44) and Compton Acres (page 47). The fifth exit is the A35 Poole Road which leads after ½ mile to St Aldhelm's Road on the left.

It is likely that the land on which St Aldhelm's church is built was given by Henry Bury after discussions with Rev. Morden Bennett, the first vicar of St Peter's church in Bournemouth, since the latter used to come to the area to preach before the area had its own church. The church was built between 1892 and 1912, although a tower planned to the south of the main entrance has never been built. What is most striking about the interior of the church is the tall ceiling supported on 17 slender pillars. The initial church was extended towards the west and the extent of the extension can be seen by looking at the ceiling.

St Aldhelm's church, St Aldhelm's Road, Branksome, Poole BH13 6BT. Open: Tuesday morning 10.30 - 11.30.

¼ mile further along the A35 past St Aldhelm's Road is a roundabout. Turning left (still on the A35) and the third turning on the left is North Lodge Road which leads into Leicester Road, Western Road and to the affluent *Branksome* Park area (page 14). Another ½ mile along the A35 past North Lodge Road is a set of traffic lights with St Osmund's Road on the left.

The magnificent and imposing, brick built church on the corner of St Osmund's Road, is worth stopping to look at, if only to marvel

at it from outside. It has Grade II* listing. The thin, hand-made bricks were specially made near Wareham in a range of colours from yellow, through shades of red, to brown and purple. The north transept and nave were built in 1904 in Byzantine style but the whole church was then completed between 1913 and 1916.

The inside of the church is just as splendid, although parts are in need of restoration. Of particular note are the mosaics in the pulpit and the column decorations. The church was built for the Church of England and was the first church to have a concrete roof. It was dedicated to St Osmund who was Bishop of Salisbury. He died in 1099 and was canonized in 1457.

After many years of use the church closed in 2000 due to lack of worshippers and because it was declared unsafe with the necessary repair bill given at around £1million. The church was offered for sale and was finally purchased by the Romanian Orthodox Church in 2005. Amazingly at this time no major repairs were deemed necessary. In 2005 the church was rededicated, this time to St Stephen, and was consecrated by a bishop of the Romanian Orthodox Church, although since then the church has also been used by worshippers of the Antiochian Orthodox Church. Relations between the two branches broke down and, in August 2007, the Romanian Orthodox priest walked out. The current priest, Father Iona Fodo, belongs to the Antiochian Orthodox Church.

St Stephen the Great Orthodox Church, Bournemouth Road, Parkstone, Poole BH14 8RA. Tel: 07773 277714. The church is open on Sundays between 09.00 and 18.30 and most Saturdays.

Opposite St Osmund's Road, on the other side of the A35, is Richmond Road which leads after ¼ mile, to St John's church in Ashely Road.

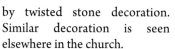

by twisted stone decoration. Similar decoration is seen elsewhere in the church.

St John's Heatherlands, Ashley Road, Upper Parkstone. Tel: 01202 717730. The church is open on the second Saturday of each month from 10.00 - 12.00.

St John the Evangelist Church, to give it its full name, was built in 1902/3, the original 1880 church having become too small. Its five east-side windows have elaborate decoration. However it is the inside of the church which is most interesting and which is the main reason for the church's Grade II listing. The beautiful timber roof was refurbished around 50 years ago. The plain circular pillars made from Cosham Down Bath stone are topped with delicately carved baskets, over which are beasts at each corner. The beasts include doves and symbols of the four Evangelists, namely the eagle of St John, the lion of St Mark, the angel of St Matthew and the bull of St Luke. The inspiration for these came from St Sophia, Constantinople. Over the arches are stone wreaths. On either side of the altar are the ten commandments carved in stone and bordered

Returning to the A35 and turning right leads, after another ½ mile, to Mansfield Road on the right, along which is the Grade II listed water tower that once served Parkstone. Continuing further along Mansfield Road leads into Victoria Road, at the end of which is Branksome Cemetery.

Branksome Cemetery is on a small hill overlooking Branksome and Upper Parkstone. The cemetery keeper's lodge and the stone built chapel were built in 1904, when the cemetery was established.

11

The cemetery chapel

The cemetery keeper's lodge

The chapel is now little used as there are no longer any spare burial plots.

Returning back along Mansfield Road to the A35 and turning right leads after another ½ mile to a set of traffic lights. Turning right and bearing left into Church Road leads to St Peter's church, a short way along on the left.

Initially Parkstone was part of the parish of Canford Magna but became a separate parish in 1833, with St Peter's being the mother church, and including the present parishes of St Osmund's and All Saints, Branksome. At that time, the church was no longer large enough, so a new church was built between 1876 and 1878 and then further enlarged until the inside was finally completed in 1901. However the planned spire was never added since Lady Wimborne withdrew the funding when she learnt the church was 'high church'; she instead gave the money to build another church, St Luke's, which is evangelical. To mark the centenary of the parish, a south porch was added in 1933 and its frieze has the carved figures of six English saints. Lord Baden Powell at the age of 55 married 23 year old Olave St Clair Soames from Lilliput in the church in 1912. Their son was christened there two years later. St Mary's church on Brownsea Island, where Baden Powell held his first scout camp, lies within St Peter's parish.

Parr Street, which leads up to the church from the A35, is named after St Peter's first vicar. On the west side of the road is the old St Peter's Primary School dating from 1833.

Returning to the traffic lights and continuing along the A35 leads, after ½ mile, to a gyratory system round Poole's Law Courts, police station and Civic Centre. The second exit is Sandbanks Road, which leads after ¾ mile to Elgin Road on the left (and the entrance to Parkstone Cemetery), after 1¼ miles to Lilliput and Salterns Way on the right, after 2 miles to Brudenell Avenue on the left (whose house prices were recorded as being the highest in the South West of England), after 2½ miles to Sandbanks Hotel, after another ½ mile to the main car park, after a further ½ mile to the Haven Hotel and finally to the vehicular ferry to Studland (see page 45).

Until a few years ago, Parkstone Cemetery had a wooden chapel, built at the time the cemetery was established. Unfortunately due to its state of disrepair it had to be demolished.

Lilliput owes its name to the fact that Jonathan Swift lived in the area at the time he wrote *Gulliver's Travels*. The main point of interest for visitors is the 285-berth Salterns Marina and the 3* Salterns Harbourside Hotel. The marina has views to Sandbanks, Brownsea Island and Poole. The hotel has a pleasant outside area overlooking the marina.

Salterns Harbour Hotel, 38 Salterns Way, Lilliput, Poole BH14 8JR. Tel: 01202 707321

The Civic Centre

Continue round the gyratory system, keeping to the left. Turn left (the Civic Centre is on the right) onto the A350, following the Town Centre sign. The entrance to **Poole Park** (page 16) is immediately on the left. There is car-parking in the park as well as roadside parking further along the A350.

Keep following the sign to the Town Centre and after a further 1½ miles you come to the George Roundabout. Turn left for the Bus Terminus and Lighthouse Theatre; turn right for **Poole Stadium** (page 37), **Tower Park** (page 38) **Canford Magna** (page 54) and **Wimborne** (page 131); go straight across for car-parking, **Upton Country Park** (page 39), **Hamworthy** (page 42) and the main road out of Poole.

The Bus Terminus has recently been renovated and is at the entrance to the Quadrant shopping centre. Opposite the terminus is the Lighthouse, Poole's Centre for the Arts and the largest arts centre outside of London (Tel: 0844 406 8666). It was built in 1979 but had a multi-million pound refurbishment in 2002. Included in the refurbished building is a 1500-seat concert hall to house the Bournemouth Symphony Orchestra.

BRANKSOME PARK

Branksome Park, in the southeast of Poole and bordering Bournemouth, is one of the most affluent areas in Poole, with many properties costing millions of pounds. Many celebrities have lived in the area over the years probably the most famous being the cricketer Wilfred Rhodes who played 58 test matches for England. Queen Elizabeth I had a house here. In 1853 Charles Packe arrived in the area from Leicestershire where he had been an MP. He purchased most of the land that is now Branksome Park and planned the layout of the area, although the development of it did not happen until after his death in 1867. He was a member of Bournemouth's first local authority and built both Poole's and Bournemouth's first general hospitals for the poor. His wife, Kitty, built a mausoleum (Grade II listed) for him in 1869. She was buried in it the following year but it was another year before her husband's body was moved there. At one time the mausoleum was offered for sale to be converted into living accommodation but when no one was willing to purchase it, it was used for storage. It gradually fell into a state of dereliction until Poole Council purchased if for a nominal £1 in 1991 and subsequently restored it. The mausoleum is on the left of the road leading to the car park in Branksome Dene Chine.

At the boundary roundabout (see page 10) take the 3rd exit (The Avenue). After 0.4 miles turn left into Tower Road. After another ⅓ mile the road bears right into Pinewood Road and the car park is ½ mile on the left.

On the death of Mrs Packe the 750 acre estate was purchased by Francis and Henry Bury who then divided the land into plots of at least one acre on which could be built a large villa. He placed covenants on the land to prevent the characteristics of the area from being altered. Henry Bury paid for the building of the church of All Saints (Grade II listed) with the foundation stone being laid by him in 1875. However he died the following year and never saw the building completed. His was the first burial to take place in the churchyard with his body having been transferred from its previous location. The church is relatively simple and small since it was primarily intended for Bury's estate staff. Its reredos depicts the last supper and is carved from a single piece of stone, whilst the organ is a memorial to those killed in the First World War.

The mausoleum can be viewed by appointment. Tel: 01202 261306. Nearest post-code is BH13 6JS

The font dates from the thirteenth century and is the oldest item in the church. The Bury family's names appear at the bottom of the stained glass windows and their graves are at the east end of the graveyard with a large stone plinth and cross commemorating them. The cypress trees lining the path leading to the cross were imported from China soon after the church was built.

Church of All Saints, Western Road, Branksome Park, Poole. BH13 6JP.

From the mausoleum continue along Pinewood Road for 200 yds and turn right into Westminster Road. After ¼ mile bear left continuing along Westminster Road. Cross over The Avenue into Tower Road West and at the end of the road turn left. The church is 100 yds on the left.

Much of the area is now a conservation area although the houses do not have listed status. Many of the properties are built at an angle to the roads and can only be glimpsed through the trees and other vegetation. Those that can be seen show the individual nature of the buildings and what was in fashion at the time they were built. One of the best known buildings is the recently built 'Thunderbird' on

'Thunderbird'

Western Avenue – directly opposite All Saints' church – which has won many architecture awards. The area is referred to in the poems of both Sir Walter Scott and Sir John Betjeman.

In 1892 the young Winston Churchill fell 30 feet from a bridge in either Alum (according to Bournemouth) or Branksome (according to Poole) Chine! It is not clear which of the chines the bridge was in since both chines were close to where Winston was staying. However most independent observers believe it was the bridge in Branksome Chine. Winston was unconscious for three days and did not fully recover for several months.

POOLE PARK

In 1875 Lord Wimborne of Canford Magna gave 110 acres of land to Poole Corporation for establishing a 'People's Park'. The park was opened five years later by the Prince of Wales. A violent storm on the opening day destroyed the specially built pavilion and the Prince had to declare the Park open from the booking office at Poole

Station, before re-boarding his train back to London. The lake was formed when an embankment was constructed to build the mainline railway between London and Weymouth which cut off part of the bay of Poole Harbour. Since then, and over a number of years, the park has been turned into a recreation area suitable for both residents and tourists. The most recent change is that the lake now has five islands similar in shape to the main islands in Poole Harbour. The lake is salt water and a sluice is opened regularly to ensure the water remains clean. The road to the south entrance of the park goes under the railway lines and the bridge was built just wide enough to take a horse and carriage. The entrances have elaborate gates with stone eagles surmounting tops of pillars. There is a lovely cottage at the north entrance.

The lake has a wealth of aquatic birds including many ducks, swans and Canada geese – the latter can number in excess of 500 at peak times. The geese were introduced to the park in the 1950s and their main food is the grass. However they produce droppings every

six minutes and this creates serious problems for the park keepers in trying to keep the grass and pathways clear. There are demands for them to be culled. Visitors are requested not to feed them.

A miniature railway, close to the cricket pitch, has been running since 1959. Initially it was feared that it would not only spoil the tranquillity of the park but also disturb the wildfowl. The ¾ mile, 10¼" track circles the freshwater lake. The first locomotive was a two-ton steam engine but the regular coal-fired steam trains stopped in 1965 in favour of diesel although it is hoped soon to purchase a new steam engine. The carriages had to be widened for Ronnie Barker when they were used for one of Ronnie Barker's TV sketches. (Tel: 07947 846262).

Poole Radio Yacht Club operates from Poole Park within a 100 x 200 metre enclosure. The depth of the lake in this region is one metre. Activities take place most days starting at 10.00 with racing on Sundays. Tel: 01202 632869. Other facilities in the park include a bowling green, crazy golf, mini pitch-and-putt, play area with swings, slides, tennis courts, and cycle track, all of which can be enjoyed by the casual visitor. A recent addition is a purpose-built boat house for the hire of rowing boats, kayaks or pedalos, or taster sessions of short courses in sailing and windsurfing. There is a one-third mile cycle track encircling the cricket pitch.

'Central Park', on the edge of the fresh water lake, houses the Cygnet Continental Café Bar, an indoor ice rink and Gus Gorilla's Jungle Playground. The playground includes a spiral slide, ball pool, drop slide, ball cannon and has a ball juggler. Both the ice rink and playground are open seven days a week from 10.00 - 18.00. In February 2009 a 12-metre high, illuminated cascade fountain was installed in the lake in front of the Mezza Luna Italian restaurant.

Poole Park, Poole, Dorset BH15 2SF. Tel: 01202 717197. No vehicular access from 06.00 - 10.00 Monday - Saturday.

For directions see page 13.

17

QUADRANT CENTRE TO POOLE HARBOUR AND QUAY

Going through the Quadrant Centre leads to the High Street and the railway crossing. Continuing over the crossing and just before North Street is Beech Hurst, which was built in 1798 by Samuel Rolles and was the last of the great mansions to be built in Poole. This red brick mansion has Grade II listing. Alongside it is Caffé Nero which, in 1923 was the Bournemouth Gas & Water showrooms. Next to Caffé Nero is the Lord Wimborne Public House.

Beech Hurst

The Public Library

Burger House

Queen Victoria's Golden Jubilee was due in June 1887 and it was suggested that a new library should be built to commemorate the occasion. The first public library, which had been built in High Street the previous year, was clearly inadequate such was the demand for its services. John Norton, who had made his money from the timber trade, offered to give £1,000 toward the new build providing that it was completed by 29 September 1887. The offer was referred to the Council's Library Committee who could not decide on a site. It was therefore referred back to full Council to make a decision but they too could

shop later sold furniture and ironmongery. When the Council had a dispute with the Gas Co. about the high cost of supplying gas for their street lights, Mr Bayley agreed to convert all the town's gas lights for use by paraffin. However they were not successful and ten years later the town reverted back to gas.

Crossing over North Street leads to the Methodist church built in 1878, although the rear chapel dates from 1793. The church is currently closed due to structural problems. A planning application has been submitted in respect of a major refurbishment, expected to cost in the region of £4 million. To pay for this, other Methodist churches in the area are to be sold.

A short way further on the left is Globe Lane. Opposite this used to be St Paul's church. The population of Poole had grown so large by the beginning of the nineteenth century that there were demands to build another church to relieve the pressure on St James's (see **Poole Cockle Trail** page 29). This resulted in St Paul's church being built in 1833; it was closed in 1956 since the congregations had declined due to the population moving away from the centre of Poole and it was finally demolished in 1963.

Further along High Street is the iconic hardware store of W.E. Boone & Co. Ltd. This Grade II listed building dates from 1820 and has changed little since that time, both inside and out!

Shortly beyond W. E. Boone the pedestrianized area ends. Turning left at the crossroads along Old Orchard leads, after a short walk, to the Poole Harbour and Quay.

not decide. By February 1887 still no site had been found but then Lord Wimborne offered to sell them a site for £100, which was agreed at the Council's March meeting. So frustrated was Norton at the time the Council was taking with still no sign of building work actually starting that he wrote to the Mayor and said that he would commence building it the following week. This he did and by using 125 workers round the clock the building was finished in time for the deadline he had previously given. The deeds transferring the land to the Council arrived one month after completion of the building! Attached to the library was an arts centre; a museum and gymnasium were added in 1890. The building is now the appropriately named Lord Wimborne Pub.

The building opposite Beech Hurst is now Burger House. It dates from the middle of the nineteenth century and was built by Mr Bayley who made his money by producing and selling brushes. His

POOLE HARBOUR AND QUAY

Poole is the second largest natural harbour in the world (Sydney in Australia being the largest) with over 100 miles of shoreline and 10,000 acres of water to explore. The harbour is the estuary of four rivers, the largest being the River Frome. It is mostly shallow, with an average depth of less than two feet, although there is a regularly dredged channel through the harbour to Holes Bay, where the Brittany vehicular ferry to Cherbourg travelled until February 2010 when it ceased operations since the route was unprofitable. However sailings recommenced in February 2011. The sand from dredging is used to replenish the beaches of Poole, Bournemouth and Purbeck. The harbour is used extensively for leisure craft. The main islands in the harbour are **Brownsea** (which is the largest with

500 acres), Furzey (owned by BP), Green, Round and the uninhabited 31 acre Long Island which was sold in 2010 to an individual for £3m.

The harbour is ideal for bird watching with Nature Reserves at **Studland** (page 59) and **Arne** (page 111) and is an important migration route for several bird species. The entrance to the harbour is only 300 metres wide and a chain ferry operates between **Sandbanks** and **Studland**. Trading vessels berth at the Hamworthy quayside, whilst fishing vessels birth at the south end of Poole Quay. Wytch Farm, on the southern shore, is the largest on-shore oil field in western Europe extracting oil at the rate of 80,000 barrels a day from beneath Poole Harbour and the sea to the south of

Bournemouth and then piping it to a terminal in Southampton. The oil was discovered in 1973 and extraction started six years later. The farm itself is carefully shielded by conifer plantations.

Poole Quay is a lively place whatever time of the day or night. There are some wonderful old buildings lining the Quay and the **Town Trail** (page 29) takes in most of them starting at the old Fish Shambles.

On the other side of the road to the Fish Shambles is the Poole Pottery outlet. Poole Pottery was founded in 1873 on Poole Quayside. The founder, Jesse Carter, realised that he had a ready source of top quality clay just north of the town and an easy means of transporting fuel in, and the finished products out, via the harbour. In the early days the pottery was famous for its tiles, mosaic flooring and other architecture products. In the 1930s the pottery started making tableware, with the first design being named the Studland and the second the Purbeck. The pottery expanded to a new site in 1999, before going bankrupt and closing in 2006. Most of the original building is now an upmarket block of flats, although part is the current retail outlet, together with a small pottery, so keeping alive the Pool Pottery brand. The company remains one of the few potteries where 100% of their pottery is made in the UK, almost equally in Poole and Stoke. Several of the Pottery's earlier pieces are displayed in the Victoria and Albert Museum as well as in **Poole Museum** (page 33). Not only can you purchase the finished products but you can also see the world famous pottery being made by the sole potter Alan White. Alan, who has appeared many times on television, including six times in the *Generation Game*, was born in Poole and has worked at the pottery for more than 40 years. It takes Alan only a few minutes of throwing his clay to make each piece and in fact the quicker the better since water has to be continually added and a piece will soon become sloppy if not completed at speed. After shaping the article is fired before being sprayed for glazing. The depth of glaze and all-over consistency is vital if the appearance and quality of the final product is to be of the required standard. The article is then fired again before being decorated. Having seen how apparently easy it is, visitors can then try their hand at making and decorating an article themselves.

Poole Pottery Studio, The Quay, Poole, Dorset BH15 1HJ. Tel: 01202 668681. Open: Monday to Saturday 09.30 - 18.00 (until 2000 on Tuesday, Thursday and Friday) Sunday 10.30 - 16.30.

Next to Poole Pottery is the historic former Swan Inn, now the Ginger Pop Shop. It is thought that there was an alehouse on this site as long ago as 1789 but the present, green-tiled building, dates from 1906. The ground floor is now dedicated to the work of Eileen Soper who was the illustrator for more than 150 of the books of Enid Blyton and of Lewis Carroll's *Alice in Wonderland*. There is a shop and an activities area which is accessed via a secret passage and includes a small but excellent mirror maze.

Open from 10.00 until 17.00 in winter and dusk in summer. Tel: 01202 670504.

The quay to the east of the old Fish Shambles leads to a mooring for pleasure boats and then the old Life Boat Station. The headquarters of the Royal National Lifeboat Institution is in Poole and in 1975 they converted their lifeboat station, built in 1882, into a small museum. The *Thomas Kirk Wright* is one of Poole's old lifeboats which was first launched in 1938 and last used in 1962; it is now on permanent loan from the National Maritime Museum. She took part in the evacuation of Dunkirk in 1940 and had to be towed home since she was badly damaged. This is one of only two remaining Surf class lifeboats in the world. Over the years the Poole lifeboat crews have been awarded 22 awards for gallantry, including one Gold and four Silver Medals. In 2008 Poole was the busiest lifeboat station in the South West with crews being launched 156 times during the year and 213 people being rescued. They currently have two lifeboats, one permanently launched and the other based on-shore. The current lifeboat station is at the western end of the quay, near the swing bridge.

The RNLI Headquarters based at West Quay Road, Pool BH15 1HZ has a small museum with a collection of replicas, cards and gifts. Open Monday to Friday from 09.00 - 17.00. Pre-booking is essential (01202 662228).

The quay in front of and to the west of the old Fish Shambles is where most of the boat tours depart (see below). Continuing west, on the opposite side of the harbour can be seen Sunseekers, the makers of luxury yachts. Further along is the swing bridge with the current lifeboat moored at the quayside.

During the summer the land train starts from the quay and arrives back after a 45 minute ride, taking in Poole Park and the High Street. The first train leaves at 10.15 and then every hour until 16.15.

Every Tuesday from April to September there is the UK's largest motorcycle meet on the quay starting at 18.00. Every Thursday in June and July there is 'Summer Breeze' – a live music event on the quay from 19.00 followed by a firework finale. In August this moves to the beach. Every Friday from May to August there is a car meet on the quay from 18.00. There is a different marque of car each Friday.

Cruises, including those round the harbour, up to Wareham River, to Brownsea Island, along the Jurassic Coast, to the Isle of Wight, Beaulieu River and bird-watching, are available from Greenslade Pleasure Boats (01202 631828), Brownsea Island Ferries (01929 462383), Dorset Cruises (0845 4684640) and Blue Line Cruises Ltd (01202 467882). If you wish to hire your own boat then try Purple Pelican (01202 687778) based in Cobbs Quay Marina (maximum of six adults). Superhawk Marine (01202 56678) run half day or evening cruises with skipper, for a boat taking up to 12 passengers. Casterway Boat Charters (01202 749 122) organise half and full day fishing charters, complete with skipper. They also run RYA training courses. For fishing charters, try also Ocean Blue (01202 67597). (Apparently the EU is planning to cap the number of fish that can be caught by these fishing charters for fear that the waters are being over-fished!) For sailing boat hire with crew try Puffin Charters (01202 667050). Brittany Ferries offer day trips to France sometimes from as low as £5 return with departures from Hamworthy (see page 23) (0871 2441498 or 0871 244 1400). Also from Hamworthy are the Condorferries' evening cruises to Jersey or Guernsey with up to four hours on shore (0845 6091030).

RNLI Lifeboat Museum, The Old Lifeboat House, Fisherman's Dock, Poole, Dorset Tel: 01202 663000. Open: Easter to end of September 10.30 - 16.00. The museum is run by volunteers so there may be times when it is not open. Free admission.

Several buses go from Bournemouth to Poole, eg m1 and m2. All terminate at the bus station, in front of the Dolphin Centre. To reach the quay, walk through the Dolphin Centre and along the main High Street which passes over a level crossing and on to the quay, passing Poole Museum. By road, join the Wessex Way and follow the road signs (see page 10).

BROWNSEA ISLAND

There have been settlements on Brownsea Island for more than 2500 years. In the ninth century a small chapel was built but was destroyed by the Vikings in 1015. In 1530 Henry VIII took control of the island and had a castle built which was to play a prominent role in the defeat of the Spanish Armada. From 1650 until the middle of the nineteenth century the island had a number of owners but then in 1852 it was bought by Col William Waugh who, together with his wife, established a pottery and built a small village which included the church of St Mary the Virgin, which was built in 1854. Unfortunately the Brownsea clay was not of high quality and the business collapsed and the couple fled to Spain with large debts. New owners continued with the pottery and also developed the agricultural side of the island. They had a love of art and filled the castle with Italian Renaissance sculpture. The castle was destroyed by fire in 1896 but was rebuilt a few years later.

The island was next bought by Charles van Raalte in 1901, after which it experienced a period of great prosperity. One of the visitors to the island was Marconi and van Raalte's children spent hours

The enclosed family pew has a fireplace

*St Mary the Virgin,
Brownsea Island*

The tomb of Charles van Raalte

sending morse messages to him by the new wireless method when he stayed in the Haven Hotel on Sandbanks. Charles van Raalte died in 1908 and is buried beneath a white marble tomb in Brownsea church. His wife kept the island for several more years before selling it to Mary Bonham-Christie in 1927, who was completely opposed to all blood sports including fishing. Farm animals were allowed to roam freely and all visitors banned – the island soon reverted to natural heathland. In July 1934 a fire broke out which raged for more than a week. Although the castle and church were saved, many of the animals perished. Mary Bonham-Christie died in 1961 at the age of 96 and the Treasury accepted the island in lieu of death duties; the island became the responsibility of the National Trust.

In 1907 Baden-Powell was invited to hold a camp on the island for his recently formed scout troop. The success of the camp led to the development of the international scout movement and today the movement still has strong links with the island. There is a commemorative stone in the south-west corner of the island, where the camp took place, a statue close to the entrance and another on Poole Pier close to the ferry departure point.

Brownsea Island, like most of the islands in Poole Harbour, is one of the few remaining habitats of our native red squirrel. After the grey squirrel was introduced to the UK, the red squirrel population declined as a parasite carried by the grey squirrel is fatal to the red squirrel. Luckily the grey squirrel has not managed to find its way to Brownsea Island. Red squirrels are very shy creatures and so are difficult to see. The best time to try is in the early morning when they come out to feed on their main staple of pinewood cones.

Brownsea Castle

The villa, orginally the island's vicarage.

There are estimated to be about 200 of them on the island.

In 1896 Japanese Sika deer were introduced to the island but were driven from it by the fire in 1934. Since the 1970s they have begun to swim back from the mainland. They are difficult to spot due to their shyness. Another species that has made a comeback is the brown long-eared bat which is now thriving, thanks to the work of volunteers.

The lagoon on the island was reclaimed from the harbour in the 1850s but during the ownership of Mrs Bonham-Christie was neglected and turned into a non-tidal wetland with hosts of birds, in particular a large number of shelduck and herons. The lagoon is now home to thousands of wading birds, including over 1000 avocet and hundreds of blacktailed godwit. There are plenty of viewing hides around the lagoon.

The villa, reached by walking along the path to the east of the church, was built as the island's vicarage, although it was never used as such. It is now used by the Dorset Wildlife Trust and has a small exhibition area.

Note that Brownsea Island is part of the Purbecks and not part of Poole.

Brownsea Island, Poole Harbour, Dorset BH13 7EE. Tel: 01202 707744. Open: Daily from March to October. ½ hourly ferries depart for the island from Poole Quay and Sandbanks and less frequently from Bournemouth Pier and Swanage.

POOLE COCKLE TRAIL

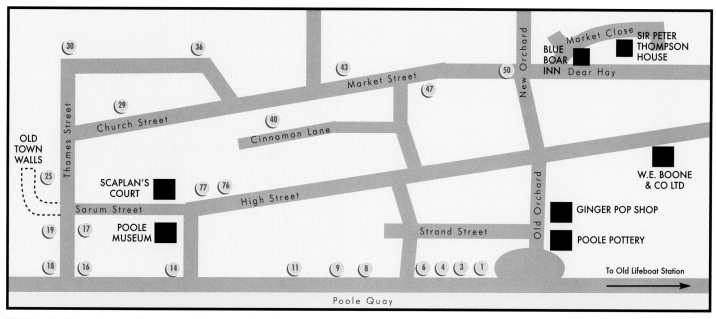

The buildings that make up the old town of Poole really are a pleasure to behold as they are so varied in design. The trail described here is known as the Poole Cockle Trail and a booklet giving full details of the buildings in the trail can be purchased from the Tourist Office which is located near the start of this trail. The numbers in this text refer to the corresponding plaques, which are set in the ground outside the relevant building. The trail starts at the site of the old Fish Shambles (1) where fish markets were held in the past.

To the west along the quay is the Lord Nelson (3) (built in 1764) and the Jolly Sailor (4) pubs. The Lord Nelson used to be known as the Blue Boar but was renamed in 1810 following the death of Nelson five years earlier.

The building housing the Oriel Restaurant (6) was once the Seaman's Mission and had a chapel on the first floor.

A short way past the Poole Tourist office is the oldest building on the Quay, the Poole Arms (8), part of which dates back to the seventeenth century. The front of the building is covered with tiles from the original Poole Pottery factory, known at the time as Carter's of Poole.

The small but beautiful Portsmouth Hoy (9) is named after the Portsmouth coasters which used to moor in this part of the harbour. The Purbeck Pottery showroom (11) is in what was once a warehouse. They started manufacturing stoneware pottery in 1966.

Crossing High Street and on the corner is the Spotted Cow pub (14) dating from the eighteenth century.

Next is the Custom House (16), scene of a major smuggling incident in 1747 when 60 smugglers raided the building to recover their contraband that had earlier been seized by customs officers. In front of it is the town beam that was used to weigh goods to determine the amount of duty due.

Next to the Custom House are the Town Cellars (17) now part of Poole Museum. Attached to the far side is a lean-to which is the old

Poole Gaol dating from 1820. At one time it was used as a fire station.

On the opposite side of Thames Street is the Old Harbour Office (18) built in 1822. Continuing up Thames Street, away from the Quay, you come on the left to the timber-framed King Charles Pub (19) built in the sixteenth century and named after King Charles X of France who landed here on his way to exile in 1830. Inside are the original old roof beams, panelling and fireplace. (See also Ghosts on page 34.)

20 yards past the pub on the same side is an alleyway that leads to remains of the town's old walls.

Further along Thames Street is the luxury Mansion House, now known as the Hotel du Vin (25) which was one of the many buildings built on the wealth created by trading with Newfoundland. It was built in the 1790 and it is well worth looking inside.

Continuing along Thames Street leads to St James's church (29). It was built in 1819 from Purbeck Stone and its supporting pillars are made from giant Newfoundland pine trees, in groups of four. Initially they were covered with plaster and it was not until 1911 that the plaster was removed and the pine columns rediscovered.

Opposite the church is the eighteenth century West End House (30) owned in the nineteenth century by the Carter family, the founders of Poole Pottery. Continuing round the back of the church leads to the Rectory (36) built in 1765 and then back to Church Street.

To the right are the St George's Alms Houses (40) built in the fifteenth century. Further along at 6 & 8 Market Street are Byngley House (43) (see Ghosts page 34) and Mary Tudor Cottage, which were originally one building and date from 1567.

Immediately ahead, beyond the Crown Hotel (47) is the Guildhall (50) built in 1761 and now the town's registry office.

Behind the Guildhall and crossing over New Orchard is the Blue Boar Inn on the corner of Market Close, which was built as a Wine Merchant's shop in 1720. It has three bars on three floors. The basement bar is of particular note and was clearly where the wines were stored. It has a large display of military and diving artefacts which is said to be one of the largest such displays outside of a museum. Many have been loaned to the landlord by the locals. It sells a range of real ales and has live music on Wednesdays, Fridays and Sundays.

The road to the left of the Blue Boar leads to Sir Peter Thompson House, also known as Poole Mansion. For some reason it is not part of the official Cockle Trail. The Mansion was built in 1746, although Sir Peter did not move into it for another 17 years. It was extended at the rear during the nineteenth century. The canopy over the entrance has an ornamental ceiling, scrolls and a helmet, with the Thompson arms above. The house is now used as offices.

Returning to New Orchard and turning left into New Orchard takes you past single story shops on the right that still have their Victorian frontage.

Turning right again into High Street there are a number of buildings, some of which have histories dating back 500 years. The Antelope (76) used to be a coaching inn and has a massive stone fireplace.

The Kings Head (77) had many secret passageways used by smugglers.

At the end of the Cockle Trail is Scaplen's Court and Poole Museums.

SCAPLANS COURT MUSEUM

Scaplans Court Museum is usually only open during the month of August, when demonstrations are given of domestic life through the ages. At other times of the year it is used to facilitate the town's education programme. It is Poole's best remaining medieval building and was built in the fifteenth century. If you look at the stone fireplaces you will see scratched there many initials and dates; these are believed to belong to troops who occupied the building during the Civil War, when it was known as the 'George Inn'. The history surrounding the building is not well documented but it is known that the building was used as a marriage settlement for one of John Scaplan's grandchildren in 1784; the date he first owned the building is not recorded. It was first opened to the public in 1929 after the Society of Poole Men purchased the almost derelict property and restored it. It is said to have a resident ghost.

When the building was purchased by the Society of Poole Men, so was the garden which had become overgrown and neglected over the years. When the Poole Men took it over they hired one of the foremost garden landscapers of the time to lay out the garden in Tudor style and so restored it to its former glory. The hard landscaping, formed from Spanish beach cobbles, is as it was in Tudor times.

The Museum, 4 High Street, Poole, BH15 1BW Tel: 01202 262600. Open: August only from 10.00 - 16.00. However the gardens are open during the summer period from 13.00 - 16.00. Free Admission.

One of the rooms has been laid out as a classroom, dating back to the 1930s

POOLE MUSEUM

Poole Museum has exhibits telling the story of Poole from pre-historic times to the present. The museum was opened in 1989 and underwent a major redevelopment between 2005 and 2007 with the aid of local fundraising and a Heritage Lottery Fund grant for £1.3million. The museum is set in an eighteenth century, Grade II, listed harbour warehouse, known as Oakleys' Mill, and is entered through a new glass atrium, above which is a visitor's lounge, reached via an entrance on the third floor and which offers views to the town and harbour. In the entrance itself is a early fire engine.

The pride of the museum's three floors of exhibits is the logboat dating from 295 BC; it is one of the largest surviving examples of such boats. It was discovered during dredging work in Poole Harbour in 1964 and was left where it was for a further 10 years whilst it was decided what to do with it. Now, 40 years later, it has a permanent home, comfortable in a temperature and humidity controlled environment enclosed in a glass case. The boat, carved from a single oak tree, is 32 ft (10 metres) long, would have carried up to 18 people as they plied their trade across the harbour. It is thought to have weighed 14 tonnes. The boat is of international historical importance.

Other than the logboat, the next major exhibit is the Poole Pottery display showing the early work of the pottery which concentrated on architecture products rather than, as now, domestic items such as tableware. It is the finest collection of Poole pottery in the world and occupies the entire third floor of the building.

Do not miss the small display of finds from the Studland Bay wreck on the first floor. The wreck of this small merchant vessel was discovered in 1984 and pre-dates the *Mary Rose*. There are also displays of the Baden Powell Scout Movement as well as of pirates – both those that operated on the high seas and the Poole Pirates who race at Poole Stadium (page 37).

At the far end of the ground floor and attached to the main museum is the medieval Town Cellars (Grade I listed). This scheduled ancient monument used to be the town's wool store where wool and cloth were stored prior to export. The building still has its original timber roof. It is now the Local History Centre containing a wide range of library material dating back many years.

The Museum, 4 High Street, Poole, BH15 1BW, Tel: 01202 262600. Open: April to October, Monday - Saturday 10.00 - 17.00; Sunday 12.00 - 17.00; November to March, Tuesday - Saturday 10.00 - 16.00, Sunday 12.00-16.00, Monday - Closed. The Town Cellars normally close at 15.00. Free Admission.

GHOSTS

Poole is said to be the most haunted town in Dorset with several buildings considered to house ghosts.

Scaplans Court is said to be haunted by a nurse from the 1800s, a Roundhead from the Civil Wars and a maid from the sixteenth century. The most frequent sighting is of the maid, whose name was Agnes Beard, who was murdered by three robbers in 1598, along with her mistress, although there have been no sightings of the mistress. One of the robbers was subsequently caught and hanged.

A number of buildings mentioned in the *Poole Town Trail* have reported ghosts or strange happenings. In Byngley House (43), Market Street, a number of people have become faint and have experienced a strange feeling in one of the upstairs bedrooms. The remains of a mummified cat was discovered there some years ago nailed to the floor. It was thought that this was to exorcise any ghosts which were there although if this were the case then clearly it was unsuccessful. The Guildhall has a ghost of a clerk who hanged himself in the nineteenth century.

The Crown Hotel (47), also in Market Street, has been haunted since a recent landlord converted some outbuildings. Since then sounds of a body being dragged across the floor have been heard as has piano playing for a room that has no piano. It is said that a previous landlord disposed of his two deformed children in the hayloft of one of the outbuildings.

The King Charles Pub (19) has had several reports of strange happenings, such as unexplained footsteps, disappearance of objects

and the voice of a young woman when there was nobody around.

Other places mentioned in this guide that are said to be haunted include the castle on *Brownsea Island*, said to have a ghost in the form of a large black figure. *Studland* has a ghost in the form of a White Donkey that regularly appears just before Christmas. It is said to be of a donkey that belonged to an old man who was killed and robbed by a naval deserter. The donkey ran off but is now said to return looking for its master. Other places that are regarded as haunted include the *Bovington Tank Museum* where the ghost is a German officer, *Clouds Hill Cottage* where the ghost is said to be T.E. Lawrence in Arab costume, *Christchurch Priory Church* where the ghosts are monks walking in the grounds or into the Draper Chapel, *Corfe Castle* where the ghost is a headless woman said to be Lady Bankes, *Wimborne Minster* where the ghost is a monk and Badbury Rings where the ghost is a Peeping Tom peering at young lovers in their cars – this ghost comes in the form of a small, bearded and hairy man thought to be an old warrior killed in battle on this site. Bournemouth's *Pavilion Theatre's* ghost, Emily, is said to wear a period costume and bonnet and walk around the circle parade.

For more details information on ghosts in the region, read *Ghosts of Dorset* by Peter Underwood from which much of the above information was obtained.

TOWN CRIER

There are around 200 Town Criers in the UK. David Squire has been Poole's Town Crier since 1958. He was born in Poole in 1942 and has represented the town in more than 100 Town Crier competitions, having won several of them. He has the distinction of being the longest serving Town Crier in the world.

Although Town Criers have effectively existed since ancient Greek and Roman times, the first official and formal system of Town Criers was introduced during the reign of William the Conqueror, when they also acted as the local upholder of the law. The role was often passed from father to son. Their purpose was to pass on news and instructions to the public, many of whom could neither read nor write. Traditionally they have elaborate dress, normally in the form of a red and gold robe with black breeches, black boots and a tricorn hat. They carry a hand bell to attract attention and a scroll on which is the information that needs passing on. After ringing their bell they usually shout the words 'Oyez, Oyez, Oyez!' meaning 'Hear ye, Hear ye, Hear ye', before giving their message in a clear and loud voice. Traditionally the message is ended with 'God Save The Queen/King'.

If you want to use the services of the Town Crier, for example to announce a wedding, birthday anniversary or to propose marriage, then he can be contacted on 01202 241301.

PIRATES

Harry Paye, or 'Arripay' as he was frequently known by his enemies, was Poole's most notorious pirate. He was believed to have been born in 1360 and died in 1419, operating for most of his pirate's life out of one of the islands in Poole Harbour. This was the time of the Hundred Years War with France and Harry played his part by attacking and plundering French ships, as well as those of the Spanish since they were allies of France for much of the period. Not only did he attack their ships but also their ports, from Normandy to the Bay of Biscay. In all he is said to have brought into Poole scores of ships that he had captured. How did he operate so freely from Poole? Because Harry was given leave by Henry IV to fight the King's enemies, wherever they were and he was made Vice-Admiral of the Cinque Ports!

In 1398 he sacked and burnt the towns of Gijon and Finisterra and stole a most venerated, gold crucifix. Then in 1405 he plundered and burnt around 40 villages along the French coast. Enough was enough for the French and in retaliation a combined force of French and Spanish ships sailed undetected into Poole Harbour and their soldiers burnt and sacked the town, including burning the Town Cellars, now part of *Poole Museum*. Their aim was to capture or kill 'Arripay' but in this they were unsuccessful, as Harry was away from Poole at the time. Two years later, with a fleet of 15 vessels he captured 120 French and Spanish ships and escorted them back to Poole. Part of the captured cargo was wine and the people of Poole spent the following days celebrating!

It is likely that the Old Harry Rocks derive their name from him, as do the Poole Pirates in *Poole Stadium*. There is a Poole Pottery plate in the Poole Museum dedicated to Harry.

Another of Poole's pirates was said to be Thomas Canaway, who was the first recorded Mayor of Poole. It seems that 'privateering', or 'pirating' was an acceptable and profitable way of life in Poole in the fourteenth and fifteenth centuries.

POOLE STADIUM

The Council owned Poole Stadium (also referred to as the Wimborne Road Stadium) was built in the early 1930s to provide a variety of entertainment to combat the Great Depression. Poole Town FC made it their home from then until they left due to poor attendance in 1994. Greyhound racing had been introduced in 1960 but left 30 years later to make way for a larger football pitch and then returned in 1994 when the football club departed. The stadium is mainly associated with the Poole Pirates since the speedway club was formed in 1948 when the cycle track which surround the football pitch was enlarged. The stadium now has a modern fully air-conditioned glass fronted indoor grandstand with a 440 seat restaurant and two bars.

Greyhound races are held every Tuesday, Friday and Saturday, with the first race starting at 7.30 p.m., or possibly earlier if the event is being televised. You can enjoy dinner in the Gallery Restaurant whilst watching. If you do not want a meal then there is a small entrance fee, however if you pick up one of their advertising leaflets from your hotel entrance is likely to be free.

The Poole Pirates are members of the Elite League, which is the top speedway racing league. The Pirates ride their 500cc machines round the 420 yards (384 metre) dirt track every Wednesday evening from April to October. Over the last 10 years they have been the most outstanding team in the country, winning the league in 2003, 2004 and 2008. In 2003 they won the Elite League, the Knockout Cup and the British League Cup and then repeated the feat the following year. They held their inaugural meeting in 1948 and are still the only speedway club to have worked their way up from the bottom division to the top Elite Division. You can see some memorabilia of the early days of the Poole Pirates in the **Poole Museum**.

Poole Stadium, Wimborne Road, Poole BH15 2BP. Tel: 01202 677449.

For directions see page 13.

TOWER PARK

Tower Park is a leisure complex, with numerous eating places, three miles from the centre of Poole. Facilities include the *Empire* (a 10-screen multiplex cinema Tel: 08714714714); *Phazarzone* (a high tech paintball-style guns – Monday to Friday 16.00 - 22.00, Saturday and Sunday 09.30 - 22.00 Tel: 08458 739645); *Splashdown* (a water complex for people of all ages although there is no adult swimming area. Opening times vary. Tel: 01202 716 123); *Gala Bingo* (visitors can join for free and then play on the same day. 11.00 - 23.00 Monday - Saturday and 12.00 - 23.00 on Sundays); *Monkey Bizness* (an indoor multi-activity centre with three play frames for the 0-2s, 2-5s, and 5-12 as well as a 5 metre climbing wall. Daily 09.30 - 18.00 Tel: 08458 739645); *LA Fitness* (a 17 metre pool, weights, cardio, sauna, beauty treatments, sunbeds. Monday - Thursday 06.30 - 22.00, Friday 06.30 - 20.00, Saturday and Sunday 08.00 - 18.00. Tel: 10202 714920); *Reel Time* (a gaming area with one area for the over 18's and the other for those under 18. Daily 11.00 - 22.00 Tel: 01202 716604); *Bowlplex* (24 lanes of bowling, licensed bar with large screen for all the sports action, grill. Latest arcade technology and six full sized American pool tables. Daily 10.00 till late. Tel: 01202 715907).

Tower Park, Poole, Dorset BH12 4NY. Tel: 01202 723 671

Take the A 347 off the Wessex Way to the Talbot Roundabout and then the A3049. At the Mannings Heath Roundabout turn left. The leisure complex is clearly signposted.

UPTON COUNTRY PARK

The Upton esate is one of the oldest sites in Poole, containing a Roman Road between Moriconium (Hamworthy) and Alavna (Corfe Mullen). Upton House, within the park, was built between 1816 and 1818 and is a Grade II listed building. The house was named after the ship *Upton* which was the pride of the Newfoundland trade fleet; it was built in 1787 but foundered in 1796. The house was planned to be built by William Spurrier but he died before he could do so. His son, Christopher, inherited the estate and had the house built. Unfortunately he was a spendthrift and gambler and when the Newfoundland trade declined, so did his fortunes. He sold the estate and died penniless. At that time the estate covered 1,000 acres; today it covers 100 acres. The estate was

gifted to Poole by the Llewellin family in 1957 and is now used mainly for offices, although the ground floors are open to the public, usually on alternate Sundays.

Tours of the ground floor are arranged at certain times and last for about 30 minutes. In the first reception room is a white marble fireplace said to be one of a pair (the other being black) made for Napoleon. There is another outstanding fireplace in the room which was once a chapel but was later used as a dining room. The Royal Coat of Arms on the fireback dates itself prior to the union with Scotland as it shows a lion with a dragon (representing Wales) rather than the unicorn which now appears in the Royal Coat of Arms. The purpose of the large mirror above was to reflect light into the room from the cupola. The three doors in the library are unique in that they appear to be shelves of books; the main door is curved.

*A shoreline trail starts from beyond the back of the house
and goes round the boundary of the grounds, passing some Holm
Oaks which were introduced to Britain in 1580*

Wonderful grounds and gardens surround the house with trees, shrubs and herbaceous borders. Like most large houses of its time, it had a walled kitchen garden to supply the occupants with fresh fruit, vegetables and flowers.

Upton House was the setting for one of the most famous trials in English legal history. In the early nineteenth century the house was owned by Edward Tichborne Doughty. When he died the estate should have passed to his nephew Sir Roger Charles Doughty Tichborne. However Sir Roger had sailed for South America in 1852 and on his return journey the ship was lost at sea with all hands. His mother would not accept this and advertised widely for news of her son's whereabouts. In November 1865 she received word that her son was alive and in Australia. Her supposed son arrived in England on Christmas day 1866 and was immediately recognise as her long lost son by his 'mother' and a servant. He lived off his 'mother's' wealth and was considerably in debt when she died in 1868. He tried to claim his inheritance but was denounced by other members of the Tichborne family as an impostor. His trial started in 1871at the end of which he was exposed as Arthur Orton, a butcher. He was subsequently tried again for perjury and sentenced to 14 years in prison. The two trials had lasted for just under three years, with the two closing addresses lasting two months and the judge's summing up taking another month. The jury took only 30 minutes to reach a verdict. However many people believed that he was in fact Tichborne and they started a small riot in London. Orton died in 1898. There have been books written, and films made, based on the incident.

There is a Romano-British Farm which uses techniques and materials employed by native Britons during the Roman periods, although this is only available for the use of schools.

In the centre of the park is the original stable block which is now used as the Peacock Tearoom, with the Peacock Art Gallery above. The estate's three remaining peacocks are usually seen here looking for food.

Both the tearoom and Gallery are open daily from 10.30 - 16.00 Tel: 01202 262628)

Upton Country Park, Upton, Poole. BH17 7BJ Tel: 01202 678140. Open: The grounds are open daily from 09.00 to dusk. The house is open alternate Sundays from 10.00 - 16.00. The walled garden is open every weekend from 10.00 until dusk. Tel: Friends of Upton Country Park 01202 262748. Free Admission. Guided walks can be arranged with the rangers Tel: 01202 672625.

From the George Roundabout (see page 13) take the A350 which then joins the A35. The entrance to the park is ½ mile further on.

HAMWORTHY

Hamworthy is the oldest part of Poole and was the site of an Iron Age settlement. The Romans later settled here and established a town which they called Moriconium and built a road from here to Badbury Rings (page 140). The name lives on in the Moriconium Quay.

From the George Roundabout (page 13) continue across following the signs to Poole Quay/Rockley Park/Channel Ferry. Turning left ¾ mile past the swing bridge, leads to the Ferry Terminal to the continent. (See page 23 for details of day cruises.) Turning right up Blandford Road, leads to the other parts of Hamworthy.

Little remains of the history of the area other than the row of four houses (Nos. 5-11), the single house (No. 19) at the start of Blandford Road (which all date from the nineteenth century) and, further on (at No. 158), the old Manor House (later the rectory)

No. 19

which dates from 1605. During the Civil War, one floor of the Manor House was used as a hospital for the Parliamentarians. Both Oliver Cromwell and the Duke of Wellington stayed here.

½ mile along Blandford Road is a set of traffic lights. Turning left into Ashmore Avenue (with Hamworthy Park at the end) leads into Lulworth Avenue, Lake Avenue and then Lake Drive with the Moriconium Quay. ⅓ mile further on is the entrance to Ham Common. Continuing on leads to Rockley Sands.

The Manor House

As you bear left into Lake Drive you pass the Lake Yard, which is part of the Moriconium Quay. The Club House has a small, although good restaurant. Lake Drive continues past the Amphibious Training Unit of the Royal Marines.

The car park at the entrance to Ham Common leads to a sandy beach with a small pier and good views across the harbour to Arne (pg 111). The first house to the east of the pier is Grade II listed and

The Boat House

known as The Boat House. It is said to be the most complete surviving modern-style house of the inter-war period in the Bournemouth and Poole area. The common itself affords pleasant walks, again with good views across the harbour.

Rockley Sands is the site of a large mobile home complex with full leisure and activities area and a café.

A further ¼ mile along Blandford Road past the traffic lights and Ashmore Avenue is Hinchliffe Road on the right which leads to Cobbs Quay.

Cobbs Quay is one of the largest quays in Poole. Of more interest to the casual visitor is likely to be the walks along the edge of Holes Bay afforded by taking almost any of the side roads leading to the Bay. The footpath alongside 145 Symes Road leads in turn to another footpath leading to Upton Country Park and Upton House (pg 39) either by the shoreline or woodland route.

A further ¼ mile along Blandford Road past the turning to Cobbs Quay is the Church of St Michael.

The original St Michael's church was razed to the ground in 1644 and the stone blocks from its walls used to strengthen the town's gates. The church was rebuilt in 1826 but unfortunately a damp-course was omitted so the church was always damp and fell into a

state of disrepair. The present church was built between 1958 and 1959 and the old one demolished in 1962, with the organ and font moved from one to the other. The only piece of the old church remaining is part of the apse which can be seen in the old graveyard beyond the war memorial. The large tomb at the rear to the right was said to have contained an Axminster carpet, together with Chippendale table and chairs. However the tomb has been broken into several times and if they were there, they are no longer. Early guide books concerning the 1826 church state that bodies of Parliamentarians killed in battle are buried in the grounds. Bearing in mind that the nearby Manor was used as a hospital, this is likely but the location of any of these graves is not known. The present church's striking reredos was a gift from the Carter pottery factory. The east window is a memorial to Lord Llewellin, who was a church warden before leaving to become the first Governor General of Rhodesia & Nyasaland.

POOLE'S BEACHES

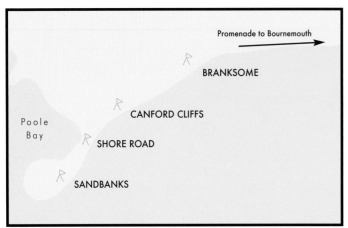

Poole has four recognised and excellent beaches, namely those at Branksome, Canford Cliffs, Shore Road and Sandbanks, although all merge into one. It is possible to walk along the promenade from the Sandbanks Hotel to **Southbourne and Fisherman's Walk**, via **Bournemouth**. There are a number of beach huts in the area. The cost of buying one is around £65,000 whilst if you want to rent one there is an eight year waiting list!

It is an easy, pleasant walk along the promenade from Bournemouth to Branksome beach and then Sandbanks. If you do not feel up to walking back you can always catch the no 50 bus for the return to Bournemouth.

The facilities at Branksome, include a licensed restaurant (closed Sunday evenings) and two shops. The restaurant was built in 1932 as a solarium where visitors could sunbath indoors; it was the first seaside resort to have one. However it was not a success and was later converted into a café and later a restaurant. On the other side of the road across from the beach, is the attractive Branksome Chine. Canford Cliffs beach has little in the way of amenities, although there is a pleasant walk down to the beach through Canford Cliffs Chine and gardens, with an array of beach huts just before reaching the promenade.

From Bournemouth, join the Wessex Way (A338). At the County Gates Gyratory, just after leaving Bournemouth, go straight across into The Avenue (second exit) signposted Canford Cliffs and Compton Acres. 1 mile further is Branksome Chine beach on the left. For Canford Cliff beach, continue for another ½ mile until you come to Canford Cliffs village. Turn left just before entering the village. After a few hundred yards the road bears right and there is a footpath that leads down to the beach.

Sandbanks Hotel

Alongside Sandbanks beach is the luxury Sandbanks Hotel (Tel: 01202 707377) from which there is direct access to the beach from its outdoor restaurant. The hotel's Brassiere has 270 degree views across both the beach and Poole Bay. The hotel operates the Watersports Academy (01202 708283) from the harbour side where you can enjoy such activities as windsurfing, kite surfing, kayaking, sailing, etc, or charter the hotel's catamaran. The Sandbanks beach is host to the British Beach Polo Championships and a Beach Volleyball Festival each July and the Animal Poole Windfest in September, which is the South Coast's biggest action sports festival.

For Shore Road and Sandbanks, continue through Canford Cliffs village and turn left at the road junction, signposted to Sandbanks. ½ mile further on, past the Harbour Heights Hotel you come to another road junction. Turn left. Shore Road is the second turning on the left, with a car-park at the end. Sandbanks Hotel is ½ mile further along the main road and a large car park another ½ mile further on.

Poole is the ideal place for participating in most water sports, either in the sea or the large sheltered harbour. There are designated areas in the harbour for some sports such as water skiing, jet skiing and water biking. The dedicated area for wind surfing and kite surfing is off Shore Road at Sandbanks. It is shallow and safe but dries out at low tide. The road is alongside the harbour so is convenient for unloading gear.

Sandbanks is the peninsula that juts out at the entrance to Poole Harbour. Properties here are said to be the fourth most expensive in the world, based on the cost per square foot. A 0.33 acre empty plot with direct access to the beach was on the market in 2009 for £13.5m.

At the southern most point of the peninsula is the luxury, four star, Haven Hotel (Tel: 01202 707333). The hotel is over 100 years old and it was from here that Marconi carried out many of his experiments with wireless telegraph and morse messages to the owner of **Brownsea Island**. Sitting in the terrace of the Harbour Hotel gives a good view of the ships going to and from the harbour, of Studland and of the chain ferry passing between Sandbanks and Studland.

To reach the entrance to the Haven Hotel, cross the mini-roundabout 100 yards past the car park and then keep to the left in the 'Ferry Lane'. The entrance is ½ mile on the left and just beyond is the Chain Ferry to the Isle of Purbeck.

There are many clubs and associations connected with water sports and most welcome the novice as well as the experienced sports person; some clubs run taster sessions. The oldest sporting club in Poole claims to be the Poole Amateur Rowing Club which was founded in 1873. Their clubhouse is just west of the Poole lifting bridge. In 1997 two members entered a competition to row across the Atlantic from Tenerife to Barbados. They took just over 60 days and finish 8th out of the 29 crews who entered. Other clubs include Poole Yachting Association (01202 741455), Poole Yacht Racing Association (01202 679561), Poole Harbour Canoe Club based in Hamworthy and Hobie Cat Centre (01202 671661).

Safaris, tours and excursions for both the novice and experienced person are organised by Jetski Safaris Ltd. (07803 620650), catamaran cruises by Haven Hotel (01202 708283) and windsurfing, kayaking and kite surfing by Poole Harbour Watersports (01202 700503).

There are a number of diving attractions, from marine life at 'The Pinnacle' to an ancient forest at 'Poole Patch'. What is more likely to be of interest to the diver are the large number of wrecks, the most famous of which is the fifteenth century *Studland Bay* discovered in 1984. There are also wrecks of merchant vessels, warship, aircraft and seven tanks! Contact 01202 580065.

COMPTON ACRES

The 10 acre Compton Acres gardens date from the 1920s when Thomas Simpson purchased acres of wild heather and gorse land together with a house with the dream of recreating the many gardens he had seen on his world travels; he invested what today would be around £10 million pounds in realising his dream. He imported many of the plants direct from their home country. Indeed everything in the Japanese garden was imported from Japan and, as the garden was designed by a Japanese gardener, it claims to be the only true Japanese garden outside of Japan. The gardens were first open to the public in 1953, after having been restored following neglect during the years of the Second World War. There have been many owners since then. Today the gardens are claimed to be amongst the finest gardens in Europe and have an international reputation, lovingly cared for by their present owners Mr & Mrs Merna.

The gardens consist of a number of themed gardens each independent of the others. These include a Roman Garden dating from 1985, an Italian Garden parts of which date back to 1924 and a Heather Garden. Planning permission has been granted to erect a £4 million, three storey, 36 bedroom hotel with a 18 metre tower on which will be planted trees. It will be similar to the Torre Guinigi tower of Guinigi Palace at Lucca in northern Italy, which was built at the end of the fourteenth century.

For the youngsters there is a model railway exhibition for which there is a small additional charge.

From 2009 the gardens are offering a series of workshops, demonstrations and lectures by experts on selected days throughout the year. For further information and dates contact 01202 426143

Compton Acres, 164 Canford Cliffs Road, Poole, Dorset BH13 7ES. Tel: 01202 700778. Open: March to October 09.00 - 18.00 and November to February 10.00 - 16.00. Shop, coffee shop and excellent restaurant.

Either side of the paths in the Winter Garden are stone statues designed and created by the Shoina tribe in Zimbabwe.

From Bournemouth, join the Wessex Way (A338). At the County Gates Gyratory, just into Poole, go straight across into The Avenue, (second exit) signposted Canford Cliffs and Compton Acres. Just under 2 miles, soon after passing through Canford Cliffs village there is a T-junction/mini-roundabout. Turn right and the gardens are ¼ mile on the left.

BOURNEMOUTH TO MERLEY HOUSE

Take the A338 Wessex Way, Ringwood Road, to the East. ½ mile beyond the speed limit de-restriction sign turn left on the B3073, signposted Bournemouth Airport. After 100 yards turn right and continue for another ½ mile to the roundabout. Turn left (first exit). Continue for 2½ miles to the next roundabout (passing the Airport, Adventure Wonderland and the Aviation Museum) and turn left. Continue along the B3073 for 2½ miles to the roundabout. Turn left and then immediately right at the next roundabout. After ¾ mile turn right along Stapehill Road (signposted Knoll Gardens). The gardens are just over ½ mile on the right.

The four-acres Knoll Gardens are delightful and contain more than 5,000 plant species. To fully enjoy the range of trees and shrubs the gardens should be visited in each of the four seasons. The gardens have an international reputation and are the UK's leading ornamental grass specialist, having won Gold Medals in the Chelsea Flower Show every year since 2002. They first appeared on the BBC TV's *Gardener's World* in 1988 and have appeared many times since. At the adjacent nursery many of the various grasses are on display and available for visitors to buy.

The gardens were started in the 1970s on a rather overgrown site that was once a market garden and nursery known as 'The Knoll'. Initially the garden was called the 'Wimborne Botanic Garden' and specialised in Australasian plants; many of the trees date from this period. However in 1988 the garden's new owners changed the name to Knoll Gardens and introduced the Water and Dragon Garden.

The sculpture in the centre of the Dragon Garden is worthy of note. It was commissioned in 1991 and is based on a legend about St Dunstan, the patron saint of Goldsmiths whose emblem is a harp. The legend describes how the devil tried to tempt St Dunstan as he worked. When the devil's gossiping became too much, St Dunstan struck the devil on his nose with his red hot tongs. The sculpture shows St Dunstan as part of the harp – the water jets form the harp's strings. He holds his tongs and the devil, in the form of a dragon, licks his burnt nose.

Follow the directions to Knoll Gardens and continue for another ½mile. Turn left at the junction. 200 yards on the left is the drive that leads to Stapehill Abbey.

Stapehill Abbey is a magnificent Cistercian abbey, known originally as the Holy Cross Abbey. It opened in 1802 and was the home of a Trappist Order of Nuns who were pledged to a vow of silence. There was no heating, even during the coldest winters, and their diet consisted of bread and beer twice a day. They arose at 2 a.m. to pray. The nunnery closed in 1989. The Grade II listed building is set in 87 acres of land. The present owners who have been carefully and sensitively restoring the property over the past 20 years now wish to sell and retire. However as yet nobody has come forward to purchase the building who is willing to continue with the work the present owners have started. The building is now empty and the farm animals have been sold, as have all the exhibition and museum items. The building and what were its award winning gardens are expected to remain closed to the public for the foreseeable future although you can travel up the drive and view the outside of the building. The small cemetery near the start of the drive is where the nuns were buried.

Stapehill Abbey, 276 Wimbourne Road West, Wimborne, Dorset BH21 2EB. Tel: 01202 861686.

Knoll Gardens, Stapehill Road, Hampreston, Wimborne, Dorset BH21 7ND Tel: 01202 873931. Open: May to mid-December, Tuesday to Sunday 10.00 - 17.00. February to April, Wednesday to Saturday 10.00 - 16.00. Closed mid-December to January. Small café area.

Continue for ½ mile past Stapehill Abbey to the roundabout and take the second exit (A31). After 2 miles go direct ahead into Merley House Lane; Merley House is ½ mile at the end of the lane.

POOLE TO MERLEY HOUSE

From the George Roundabout (pg 13) take the B3093 to Wimborne. After ¾ mile it joins the A35 and (after another ¼ mile) the next road on the right is Dorchester Road which leads, almost at the end of the road, to Poole's main cemetery.

The land for the Dorchester Road Cemetery was given to the town in 1854 by John Garland and a small commemorative stone is on the right near the entrance. Like many business men at

that time, Garland was involved with the fish trade and spent much of his time in Newfoundland. He was elected Mayor of Poole in 1824. Of the two chapels in the cemetery, the first one reached is un-consecrated and is now used as a store, whilst the other, almost identical apart from the cross on its top, is rarely used since the cemetery has few spare grave plots. In the Catholic part of the cemetery (to the left as you enter) are the headstones to two Belgian soldiers who died during the Second World War. The cemetery was laid out by Christopher Crabb Creek, who also laid out Bournemouth cemetery.

Belgian graves

Continue to the roundabout and return to the A35 and join the A349 (Wimborne Road). Continue on the A349 for 2 miles to the Dunyeats roundabout. Turn left and a short distance along on the right is the entrance to the peaceful Broadstone Cemetery.

Broadstone Cemetery has a narrow drive leading to it and then an avenue of conifers. Soon after entering, on the right, is the grave of Alfred Russell Wallace. Wallace was born in 1823 and spent much of his early life in South America, Indonesia and Malaysia. He proposed the theory of evolution while on his travels in Gilolo before and independent of Charles Darwin. However Wallace was relatively unknown whereas Darwin was a prominent scientist and although a prolific author himself (he wrote 22 books and more than 700 articles), he encouraged Darwin to write his book 'On the Origin of the Species'. The two were close friends and Darwin was instrumental in having the government award Wallace a £200 per year pension for his lifetime work in science. Wallace's fame spread and he is now regarded as one of the most prominent scientists of the nineteenth century. Wallace moved to Broadstone in 1902 and on his death at the age of 90, his wife arranged for him to be buried in Broadstone as he had requested, rather than in Westminster Abbey as his supporters wanted. His grave is uniquely marked with a fossilised tree, said to have been brought back by Wallace from his travels.

A few hundred yards further along Dunyeats Road on the left is Water Tower Road which leads, as its name suggests, to a Grade II listed Water Tower.

Return to the A349 and turn left. At the second roundabout turn left into Merley House Lane. Merley House is ½ mile at the end of the lane.

The grave of Alfred Wallace

MERLEY HOUSE

Merley House was built for Ralph Willett between 1752 and 1760. It is one of fewer than 250 Grade I listed houses in England. The three-bay projecting centre is faced with Portland stone. A walled garden on the north east of the house and an orangery on the south were added. Willett was a great collector of books and pictures and, in 1772, two wings were built on to his home to house his ever increasing collection. The wings were connected to the main house by two curved colonnades. By all accounts the library was outstanding with carved mahogany bookcases each with an ornamental scroll inscribed with the subject of the books (many of them rare) it shelved. The plasterwork on the ceilings indicated the progress of civilization. On Willett's death in 1795, the estate passed to one of his cousins. The Willett's wealth was based on the West Indian sugar industry and the slave trade and with the end of the sugar monopoly and the abolition of the slave trade at the start of the eighteenth century the family fortune collapsed. The great library of books and pictures were auctioned in 1813 and the two wings demolished leaving the house as it stands today.

What makes Merley House outstanding is the interior. The staircase is considered one of the finest staircases of its type in England. The hand rail is veneered lignum vitae, which is the hardest wood known to man and which sinks in water.

Even more impressive than the staircase and what the house is justifiably famous for are its plasterwork ceilings which are magnificent. That in the south-west Drawing Room is predominately green. The large oval panel in the centre depicts the Judgement of Paris.

The Dining Parlour is decorated in blue-grey tones and the central panel of the ceiling depicts the Roman god of wine, Bacchus, receiving a cup of wine from the Roman goddess of the harvest, Ceres.

The Morning Room is decorated in a shade of grey and the ceiling, almost unbelievably, is made from papier-mâché!

Since the two wings were demolished, the house has changed owners several times. A caravan park was started in 1960 to help pay for the restoration of the house which at that time was in a dilapidated condition. At the end of the last century the house was home to an outstanding collection of more than 5,000 model cars. Today the ground floor rooms are hired out for conferences and wedding ceremonies, although the sign at the start of Merley House Lane still implies that there is a model museum there, even though this closed at the end of the twentieth century.

The interior of the house is not generally open to the public but, along with the walled garden and the Orangery, can be hired for weddings, conferences and events. The outside can be viewed at any time.

Merley House, Merley House Lane, Wimborne Dorset BH21 3AA Tel: 01202 848099.

CANFORD MAGNA

Although Canford Magna is in Poole, it is conveniently visited when combined with a visit to Wimborne. The places of interest are the school, church and old village.

Canford School used to be Canford Manor and was mainly built in the nineteenth century, although parts date from the fifteenth century. At various times it was owned by the Crown, normally a result of the then owner supporting the loosing side when the Crown was in dispute. In 1846 Sir John Guest, who made his money from iron-founding in Wales, in particular from making railway lines, purchased the house on the site together with 17,000 acres that extended to the sea in what is now Poole and enlarged it into a mansion. The house included an exhibition room for displaying his Assyrian treasures, most of which have since been sold to the Metropolitan Museum in New York. The boy's public boarding school that purchased the school in 1923 discovered, in 1994, that a frieze in the school's tuck shop was an original taken from the throne room

Canford church

The Lodge

Canford church interior

of a ninth century Assyrian king, rather than as they had thought a copy. It sold at auction to the Miho Museum in Japan for nearly £8m, ten times the estimated value. There is now a copy of the frieze in the tuck shop. The money was used to build a new school theatre and improved sports facilities. The entrance to the school is through The Lodge, built in 1850. Although the school is not open to the public, glimpses of it can be seen from the church and road and school open days are held twice a year.

Canford church, which is Grade I listed, has no known dedication. It dates from the middle of the eleventh century and replaced one destroyed by King Cnut. Several monarchs from the fifteenth and sixteenth centuries are believed to have worshiped here. The church immediately strikes the visitor as being quite unusual. This is the result of different parts of the church being built over a period of 800 years. The thick walled chancel is the oldest part of the church dating from 1050, the main part of the nave dates from the start of the thirteenth century which is when the tower was also built; the two aisles are from the fourteenth century and the nave's extension from 1876. The fine stained glass windows at the chancel's eastern end date from 1855 and depict Matthew, Mark, Luke and John, with Christ in the centre. The beautifully carved choir stalls vary in size and were custom made for the various members of the Guest family. The marble tomb immediately outside the church's entrance is that of Sir Henry Layard. As the tomb states, he is credited with the discovery of Nineveh of which Nimrud formed part and which is now in modern day Iraq. Nimrud was the capital of the Assyrian empire for about 1000 years. Layard carried out excavations in Nimrud and brought some of the items to England which are now in the British Museum. Such was the weight of the items that it required a team of 300 men to tow the wagon on which they were placed. Sir Henry is buried here because he married Sir John Guest's daughter.

Canford Magna parish church, 2 Chichester Walk, Merley, Wimborne BH21 1SN. Tel: 01202 887733.

The school is on the banks of the River Stour and a footpath leads from it to Wimborne. A short way along the path is the Canford Suspension Footbridge. It is the only one of its type in the country and was erected by Sir John Guest. As visitors cross the swaying bridge, they have clear views of the river.

At the far end of the footpath is the beautiful Grade II listed Wimborne Lodge built in the middle of the nineteenth century and which was at one of the original entrances to the Canford Estate. (The lodge can also be reached by car along Oakley Hill and is on the right just before crossing Canford Bridge.) At that entrance to the footpath is an old turnstile with the inscription "foot passengers only cycling strictly prohibited". The Grade II listed Canford Bridge dates from 1813, although the arches date from 1675.

On the death of Sir John Guest in 1852, he was succeeded by his

Wimborne Lodge

eldest son, Sir Ivor Bertie Guest, who in 1880 became the first Lord Wimborne. Under Sir John there had been few cottages for estate workers but Sir Ivor's wife organised the building of a model village. One common feature to all the buildings in the village was the elaborate chimneys. Just as you leave the village, at the road narrow restrictions and opposite one of the school's entrances, is a narrow lane leading to the small Canford Cemetery. Among the headstones there is one to a son of Sir John Guest.

From Merley House, return to the A439 and turn right. After 200 yards turn left at the roundabout onto the B3073. After a further 300 yards, just past the public house, turn right into Oakley Lane and the lane to Canford church and school is 1 mile along on the left. Canford Magna village is reached by continuing along Oakley Lane.

ISLE OF PURBECK

The Isle of Purbeck is not an island but a large peninsula. In December 2001 part of the southern coastal region of England was recognised by UNESCO as one of the natural wonders of the world. The region, referred to as the 'Jurassic Coast', starts on the outskirts of Swanage and continues to Exmouth in the west, a distance of 95 miles. The coast has some spectacular and unsurpassed scenery with such outstanding views as Durdle Door, Lulworth Cove and the Old Harry Rocks. The glorious sandy beaches are perfect for relaxing, the crystal clear sea perfect for swimming and the miles of footpaths a few hundred yards inland perfect for walking. However the paths cross seven miles of military ranges and at certain times and at certain points you are not allowed access. You can see dinosaur's footprints, as well as hunt for fossils which you are permitted to keep, although you cannot hammer for them. The rocks vary in age as the ground tilted and folded to give the various formations. For example those at Studland are only 65 million years old whereas further west they are more than 130 million years old. In 2009 it was announced that fossils had been found along the coast which when pieced together formed a 7'8" skull of a sea monster that lived about 140 million years ago.

With all the glorious sandy beaches, many visitors do not realise that a mile below Studland Bay and out towards Bournemouth, is the largest oil field in Western Europe. The oil is held between the grains of sand and as it is removed water takes its place.

The National Trust has warned that due to global warming and the rise in sea levels, flooding and erosion of the coastline could seriously affect Studland and other areas. The beach huts on South Beach could be in jeopardy, as could the car park, information centre, café and shop.

The region has the only cow-girl in Britain. She patrols the National Trust land, covering over 1,800 acres. Prior to her appointment in 2008, cow herding had not been carried out in Britain for more than 200 years. She looks after the 15 Red Devon cows all day, herds them to ensure they graze all over the heath, keeps an eye open for strays and then rounds them up at dusk.

Travel a few miles inland and you find some of the most glorious small villages in the whole of Britain. Many of the villages are constructed with local Purbeck stone topped with thatched roofs. Many of the churches are a delight to see with the small St Nicholas church at Studland one of the best complete Norman churches in the country.

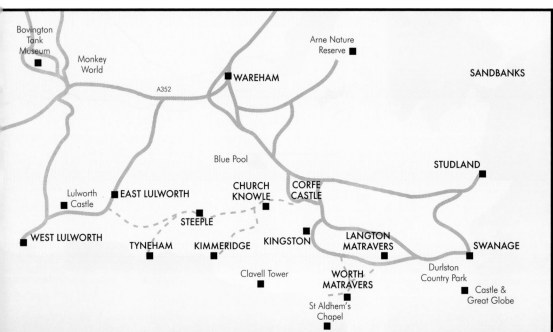

The Wilts & Dorset No. 50 bus leaves Gervis Place in Bournemouth and crosses into Purbeck by the chain link ferry. It then passes through Studland on its way to Swanage.

STUDLAND

The small village of Studland has a population of under 500 and is famous for its three beaches - Knoll, Middle and South Beach. The beaches stretch for more than three miles and are among the finest in the country, with more than one million visitors a year. They are protected by Old Harry Rocks and this has allowed a sand dune system to develop – one of the few such systems in the country. Bournemouth and Poole are losing sand (which is regularly replaced) and much of it is landing at Studland; this gives rise to the dunes. The whole area is listed as one of the top 30 nature reserves in England. Behind the sand dunes is heathland with the Little Sea, a freshwater lake which was cut off from the sea by the formation of the dunes. Legend has it that Sir Bedivere threw King Arthur's sword into Little Sea.

The sea in Studland Bay has the highest density of seahorses in the world. There is also a large number of its close relative, the pipefish. All these species have recently been declared protected and there are plans to create a protection zone for them in the bay. Seahorses mate for life and are unique in that the male gives birth to

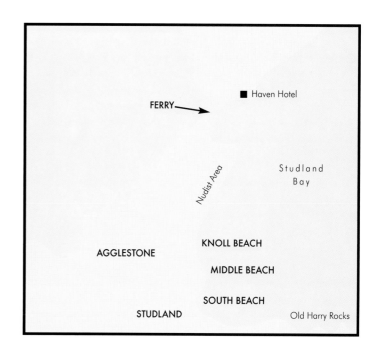

their young – the female deposits her eggs in the male's pouch, he then fertilises them and carries them for the two to four weeks of pregnancy.

A one-mile stretch of the beach has been designated by the National Trust as an official naturist/nudist beach and has been used as such for more than 90 years. The multi-colour gay flag is frequently displayed and more men than women use this beach. It is the most popular nudist beach in the country but non-nudists can also use it.

The National Trust

NATURISTS MAY BE SEEN BEYOND THIS POINT

Studland is reached by taking the vehicular chain ferry from Sandbanks which departs from in front of the Haven Hotel every 20 minutes from 07.00 until 23.00 and crosses to Shell Bay. The ferry returns from Shell Bay leaving every 20 minutes from 07.10 until 23.10. Direct access to this naturist part of the beach is reached up the footpath leading from Ferry Road Jerry's Point bus stop (No. 50 bus), which is ½ mile beyond the toll booth.

Just after leaving the ferry and before reaching the toll booth, on the right is the Shell Bay Seafood Restaurant and Bar (Tel: 01929 450363) listed in 2010 by the *Sunday Times* as one of the best places in Britain to eat by the sea. There is a National Trust car park immediately on the left after passing through the toll.

Knoll Beach has a visitors' centre with a licensed café and a National Trust Information Centre. The Trust organises walks, talks and other events which normally take place or start at the centre.

The entrance to Knoll Beach is just over 2 miles from the toll booth.

National Trust Countryside Office, Studland, Swanage BH19 3AX Tel: 01929 450259.

A ¼ mile past the Knoll House Hotel is a turning on the right leading to the Aggleston Rock. This is a 400 ton, 17ft high, block of ironstone perched high on Godlingston Heath. It used to be

The 1931 colonial style Knoll House Hotel set in 100 acres of land is on the right after you leave Knoll Beach. A stop here for coffee or lunch makes a relaxing break. (Tel: 01929 450450)

Agglestone Rock

mushroom-like but it toppled over to its present state in 1970. It is said that when the devil, who was sitting on the Isle of Wight, saw how beautiful Corfe Castle was when illuminated by the sun, he took off his hat and threw it at the castle but it fell short. The road to the rock is rough but car-worthy for about ½ mile, after which the footpath is well signposted for the final mile. It is a pleasant country walk, through woodland and heath.

Continuing on the road past the turning to Aggleston Rock for a further 200 yards, brings you to Studland Stables on the right. Studland Bay is one of the few places in the UK where you can horse

ride through the surf. There are restriction on when you can do this and permits are required. Contact Studland Stables (Tel: 01929 450273 or the National Trust 01929 450259).

2¾ miles from the toll booth or 50 yards past the stables, is Beach Road on the left leading to Middle and South Beach. The car park for Middle Beach is a few hundred yards further on, while to get to South Beach you need to immediately turn right into Rectory Lane.

On the edge of the Middle Beach car park is a small observation hut with a telescope at the top of the short flight of steps to the café, shop and beach.

The café is open 09.30 - 17.00 daily in summer and 10.00 - 16.00 at weekends in winter.

The National Trust is considering removing the rock walls that are protecting the cliffs and beach along this part of the coast and letting nature shape the coastline. If they proceed with this, then the café would be expected to fall into the sea within ten years. Looking back as you walk down to the café can be seen some of the 'dragon's teeth' that were built to stop any possible landing of tanks by enemy forces during the second world war.

Further evidence of the defences built to counter any possible invasion can be seen by joining the coastal path opposite the entrance of the car park and walking a few hundred yards along it. There you will see the gun emplacement, Fort Henry, built in 1941 and

Dragon's teeth

named after Fort Henry in Ontario whose engineers built it. The entrance to the underground munitions store is via two doors in the construction, although you are unable to gain access. The circular patch on the ground is where the 4" naval gun was installed. Visitors can however walk through the large observation building that was constructed a few years later so that the war leaders could observe the preparation for the forthcoming invasion of Europe in relative safety.

On the left as you return from the WWII defences are the grounds of the Manor House Hotel. The history of the hotel goes back to the time of King John when in 1205 he landed in Studland (or Stodlandt as it was then known) on his way to a mission in France. He later returned and built a castle. Part of the castle, namely the two round towers, remain embedded in the existing hotel. It was from the grounds of the Manor that King George VI, Winston Churchill and Eisenhower watched the invasion exercises in Studland Bay in preparation for the D-Day invasion during World War II. The thatched summer house dates from the Victorian era.

To reach the Manor House turn right into Rectory Lane. 200 yards further on is a road junction and immediately opposite is the hotel. Turn left for the hotel's car park, which is ¼ mile on the right. The hotel can also be reached by a footpath from Fort Henry.

Manor House Hotel

Still in use for worship is the small church of St Nicholas, parts of which date from the seventh century, although Roman remains from a much earlier period have been unearthed. It is built on the site of a Saxon church which had been destroyed by the Vikings on one of their many raids. Most of the building dates from the twelfth century and is one of the oldest and most complete Norman churches in the country. The enormous Norman arches are what immediately draw one's attention. A 500 year old yew tree is on the west side below which is the church's earliest known tomb dating from 1705. The tomb on the south west surrounded by iron railings is that of the Bankes family who bequeathed the Kingston Lacy estate to the National Trust.

Bankes Arms Country Inn is reputed to date from 1549, although most of the building dates from 1920. The inn has set up its own brewery, known as the Purbeck Brewery. Each August it holds a four day Beer Festival.

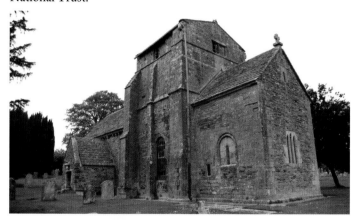

To reach the church, turn right at the Manor House along Manor Road. The National Trust car park is 200 yards on the right, just before the Bankes Arms. A footpath from the back of the car park leads to the church.

In Saxon times, free-standing crosses were places where people would congregate to worship before churches were built. The Studland Cross in front of St Nicholas' church dates from 1976 and was carved following earlier Saxon designs. The main cross is carved from stone taken from St Aldelm's Head.

Bankes Arms, Manor Road, Studland, Dorset BH19 3AU Tel: 01929 450225. Isle of Purbeck Brewery Tel: 01929 450227 (tours given by prior appointment).

The Cross is a few yards down the drive from the front gate of St Nicholas' church. It can also be reached by driving a few hundred yards beyond the Bankes Arms.

OLD HARRY ROCKS

Protruding from the end of Studland Bay are the Old Harry Rocks. They form the eastern end of the Jurassic Coast World Heritage Site. They are mainly chalk, with some layers of flint. The brilliant white colour comes about by erosion which constantly causes the outer layer to fall away. They are the youngest section of the cliffs. There is an argument about which is Old Harry but most people agree that it is the large, tall stack at the end of the ridge with the smaller stack next to it being his second wife – his first wife collapsed into the sea just over 100 years ago! The reason the rock is so named has been lost with time. Some say that it has come from 'Old Harry' – the pseudonym for the 'devil' – others that it is named after the famous pirate Harry Paye who used to hide his contraband here and others that there was once a fort here built by a King Henry.

The chalk sea-stacks known as 'The Pinnacles' are clearly visible from the cliff top overlooking Old Harry

Continue along the road in front of the Bankes Arms for about 100 yards to the public toilets. The path for the short walk to South Beach starts just before the toilets, whereas that to the cliffs overlooking the Old Harry Rocks is just beyond. The latter is a 1 mile walk over mainly smooth, level ground.

SWANAGE

Swanage is the largest town in Purbeck with a population of just over 10,000. Originally it was a small fishing port, then a centre for quarrying and now a seaside resort. The impression when entering the town from Studland along Shore Road is of a neat and pleasant seaside town; the beach on one side and the gardens on the other create a pleasing ambiance. One of its main attractions is the Swanage Railway. The Tourist Information Centre (open 10.00 - 17.00; Tel 01929 422885) is in the part of Shore Road that is closed to road traffic during the summer. Further along Shore Road is the King Alfred Monument erected in 1862 to commemorate the defeat by King Alfred of the Danes in 877 when 120 Danish ships were destroyed. The cannon balls on top of the monument were fired by the Russians at British ships during the Crimean War and became embedded in the woodwork. They were recovered when the ships had returned to port. Further along the Promenade is the small

Museum & Heritage Centre which was the Old Market Building built in the 1890s.

Further along the Promenade is the 1895 Pier which has been recently restored.

Swanage Museum & Heritage Centre, The Square, Swanage, Dorset BH19 2LJ Tel: 01929 421427. Free Admission. Open: Easter to October 10.00 - 17.00 (Closed 13.00 - 14.00).

The next turning on the right is Church Hill which leads to the Church of St Mary the Virgin whose massive church tower dates from the early seventeenth century. The turning just before the church leads to an attractive row of cottages in front of the Mill Pond. Continuing past the church leads to Kings Road West, which on turning right leads to Swanage Railway Station.

Along the path past the pier is the Wellington Clock Tower (minus the clock which had been unreliable!) that was once at the Southwark end of London Bridge – there was insufficient money to purchase the statue of Wellington! If you have driven into Swanage from the ferry then continue through the one-way system along High Street. You pass on the right, the Town Hall built in 1882, although its stone front with the iron balcony dates from the seventeenth century when it had been constructed for a building in London. Almost opposite is the imposing Purbeck House Hotel dating from

1875. It has an amazing number of items from London including a tiled floor from the Houses of Parliament which is now on the floor of the temple in the hotel's garden – the eight columns were from the toll house on Waterloo Bridge. The hotel's front façade was built from off-cuts from the Albert Memorial.

Purbeck House Hotel, 91 High Street, Swanage BH19 2LZ Tel: 01929 422872.

To reach Swanage continue on the B3351 from the ferry and 1 mile after the turning for Middle and South Beach, take the left fork signposted to Swanage and continue for 2½ miles. The road passes alongside the bay and turns sharp right, when it becomes the A351 (Victoria Avenue). The No. 50 bus goes from Bournemouth direct to Swanage, via the ferry, and stops at Swanage Station.

SWANAGE RAILWAY

The idea of a railway linking Swanage and Wareham was first proposed in 1847 but the necessary permission was not obtained until 1880. Work on constructing the 11 mile line started in 1883 and the first train left Swanage in 1885. The first plans for closing the line were in the 1950s but such was the uproar that they were dropped. The next attempt at closing it was in 1963 and, when that failed, again in 1967 when notice was given that the line would be closed the following year. The line was finally closed in 1972 and the track removed, although the track from Furzebrook to Worgret and on to Wareham was left since this was used for freight traffic in relation to the extraction of clay and for working the oil field at Wytch Farm. In 1975 a group of enthusiasts acquired the track with the aim of once more creating a public transport link to Wareham and establishing a steam and railway museum. A short length of line was opened in 1979 and since then extended so that it is now possible to travel six miles by rail from Swanage to Norden, which is about halfway to Wareham. It is also possible for trains to travel the full distance from Swanage to Wareham by using the freight line beyond Norden. On 1 April 2009 the first train since 1972 travelled from London's Victoria Station to Swanage. It is hoped that this may become a more frequent event.

The railway currently has 16 locomotives of which five steam and three diesel are operational on the line. At Swanage Station, the ticket office is the original one and the platform has been returned to its original appearance albeit with various memorabilia displayed. The ride from Swanage is through the lovely Dorset countryside with stops at Herston Halt (by request), Harman's Cross, Corfe Castle, and Norden where there is a large, free park-and-ride car park as well as the small Purbeck Mineral and Mining Museum which is open on

Sundays. (Free admission.) The journey takes one down memory lane with reminders of an era long past. If as a child you had dreamt of becoming a train driver then you can learn how to drive a steam train by joining one of the railway's courses. The railway is run mainly by volunteers and now carries over 200,000 passengers a year.

At Corfe Castle Station there is a small Swanage Railway Museum in the converted Goods Shed. As well as an exhibition there is a video detailing the history of the railway. (Free admission.)

You can enjoy dinner on the Wessex Belle – one of their dining service trains which operates on most Saturday evenings during the summer offering a five course meal. Pre-drinks are at 19.00, departure from Swanage station is at 19.30 and return to Swanage at 22.30 after two trips to Norden and back. Booking is necessary.

Swanage Railway Company Ltd, Station House, Swanage, Dorset, BH19 1HB. Tel: 01929 425800. Open every weekend from mid-February to the end of the year and every day from April to October.

The No. 50 bus goes direct from Bournemouth to Swanage Station. From Wareham, take the A351 to Norden Park where there is a free park-and-ride facility.

DURLSTON COUNTRY PARK

Anvil Point Lighthouse

The 280 acre park is home to 33 species of butterfly, over 250 species of birds, 500 wildflowers and 500 moths. The undefended high limestone cliffs provide the perfect habitat for birds and those seen will depend on the time of year; in winter there are ducks and divers from the Arctic and in summer gannets and shearwaters. The rocks in Durlston Bay date from the late Jurassic and early Cretaceous periods, which are 140 to 130 million years ago. The world famous rocks are the best source of reptile and mammal fossils anywhere in the world. The cliffs also provide a high lookout point for viewing dolphins that are frequent visitors to these waters. The park is one of the most important in the country. Dorset County Council purchased the castle and land in 1973 to form its first country park.

Durlston Castle, a Victorian folly, was built in 1886 by George Burt who made his money from quarrying and stone masonry. It is built completely of local stone. The castle is currently closed for restoration, although the Lookout Café, with wonderful views across the English Channel and to the Isle of Wight, is open. Surrounding the castle are a

Tilly Whim Caves

number of stone tablets inscribed with poetry and other facts which were of interest in the Victorian era. The globe of the world is to the south of the castle down a flight of steps. It weighs around 40 tons, is 10 feet in diameter and shows how the world was seen just over 100 years ago. Behind the globe is a stone wall with astronomical information carved into it.

The Visitor Centre, which is a short walk to the west of the castle, has a CCTV monitor which permits visitors to see the bird activity on the cliff face. The path in front and to the right of the centre leads after about ½ mile to the Anvil Point Lighthouse as well as the remains of a Napoleonic telegraph station that was erected around 1795. The Tilly Whim Caves, formed by stone quarrying can be clearly seen from the path to the south of the lighthouse. Alongside the made up footpath to the lighthouse is the entrance to a mine with the winding gear used for extracting the huge pieces of stone still in place.

Durlston Country Park, Lighthouse Road, Swanage, Dorset BH19 2JL Tel: 01929 424443 Open: Daily from sunrise to sunset. The café is open daily from April to October from 10.00 - 17.00 and at other times on Thursday - Sundays from 10.30 - 15.00. Entrance to the park is free but there are car parking charges.

The route to the park is clearly signposted from the start of the A351 and goes through the centre of Swanage.

LEESON HOUSE

Leeson Manor House is a Grade II listed building now used as a Field Studies Centre by Dorset County Council. In 2003 the centre was threatened with closure due to the large subsidy required to keep it open. However the subsidy has now been significantly reduced and hopefully the threat of closure has passed. Day and residential courses are held for students of all ages and abilities, including for those recognised as being highly gifted and talented.

There is believed to have been a house on the site for more than 1500 years which at the time of the Domesday Book belonged to the King. The present house dates from around 1808 although parts date from much earlier. The oldest part is believed to be the stone

barn which is over 500 years old. George Garland bought the house in 1816. Garland made his fortune from the Newfoundland fish trade and his Poole town house is now the Hotel du Vin (see page 30); he, along with other members of his family, is buried in Poole's main cemetery for which he gave the land (see page 50). The Garland family sold Leeson House in 1875 and from 1903 it was a girls school until the outbreak of WW II when it was requisitioned by the Air Ministry for research into Radar; it was from here that the first tracking of a submarine took place. The air raid shelters built on the site are now being used to attact the Greater Horseshoe Bat. After the war the house again reverted to a school until purchased by Bournemouth Education Centre for use as a field centre.

The Garlands introduced fine seventeenth century Italian and Flemish wood carvings into the building, some of it being from pieces of dismantled furniture which was used as panelling. The grounds extend to seven acres and include three ponds. Deer can often be seen in the grounds.

Leeson House Field Studies Centre, Langton Matravers, Swanage Dorset BH19 3EU Tel: 01929 422 126. The house is open to visitors by prior appointment.

Take Victoria Avenue (the A351) from Swanage, signposted to Wareham. After 1½ miles turn left on the B3069. Leeson House is 1¾ miles on the left.

LANGTON MATRAVERS

The village of Langton Matravers, which dates back to pre-Saxon times, has a population of just over 1000 and consists mainly of one long street. The village outskirts begin as you leave the A351, passing Leeson House (page 70) on the left. One of the first buildings on the right is Coombe Farm Cottage dating from 1900. A fire caused by a drunken farm worker overturning an oil lamp caused most of the original building to be destroyed. The farm itself is listed in the Domesday Survey of 1086.

The Ship Inn dates from 1884 while the building opposite is the Langton Matravers Farm House, which used to be the largest in the parish.

From Leeson House, continue on the B3069 for another 200 yards and the Ship Inn is on the left.

The Ship Inn

A further 300 yards past the Ship Inn is the Putlake Adventure Farm, which has a host of activities for young people. The farm is set in 30 acres and has a range of farm animals such as pigs, sheep and goats as well as owls, ponies and horses, including rare breeds. Opportunities exist to bottle feed the lambs and goats and a tractor ride round the farm is offered for an additional fee. There is an outdoor play area, as well as a large indoor heated soft play zone, which is especial useful in poor weather.

In 2007 the largest Bronze Age, axe hoard to be found anywhere in Europe was discovered in the field behind Putlake Farm. Many of the items were in almost perfect condition and were thought to have been a gift to the gods in a burial site The hoard is now on display in the Dorchester Museum.

Putlake Adventure Farm, Langton Matravers, Swanage, Dorset BH19 3EU Tel: 01929 422917 Open: Daily from 10.00 but you are recommended to phone beforehand to check, especially in winter. Tea room.

A mile past the farm on the right is the church of St George which was built in 1876, although the tower dates back to the late thirteenth and early fourteenth centuries and the list of rectors to early thirteenth century. The church is the oldest building in the village. The stone statue in the front of the grounds is of a stone mason and was carved for the millennium by Mary Spencer Watson.

Behind the church is the Museum of the Stone Industry, which is run entirely by volunteers. The museum's collection is the result of bringing together three private collections. At the Festival of Britain in 1951 they held their first formal exhibition. The collection continued to grow and a small Parish Museum was opened in 1985 where rotating exhibitions were held. However when the Quarrying

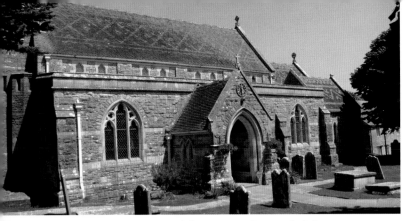

Opposite the church is the Village Hall built in 1845, which used to be the village school.

and Stone-masonry exhibition was dismantled there was outrage amongst the villagers and so a second museum was opened in the village Coach House in 1982 for the specific purpose of displaying this exhibition. The first museum closed due to the expiry of the lease on the original building but the present Coach House museum has continued.

The museum traces the history of the use of Purbeck limestone from Roman times to the present day and shows how the local stone was quarried and used. The display includes fossils, worked stone, a collection of stonemason's tools, photographs and a reconstruction of a section of underground quarrying. The total number of exhibits exceeds 25,000 although many are kept in the museum's store. Regular exhibitions of some of the stored items are held in the village hall. Such items include Victorian clothes, furniture from the local schoolroom and from the Edwardian shop, clocks dating from 1770, watches jewellery, musical instruments, medals and craft tools.

There is a nominal entry charge to the museum. A number of local booklets are for sale, including a guide to the village, the church and the villages of Worth Matravers, Corfe Castle and Kingston. Most of the booklets are written by Reg Saville, the curator of the museum, and are well worth buying. Reg is normally in attendance at the museum on Saturdays and has a wealth of local knowledge. It is hoped that a purpose-built museum can be constructed within the next two years.

Langton Matravers Museum, St George's Close, Langton Matravers, Swanage, Dorset BH19 3HE. Tel: 01929 423168. Open: April - October, Monday - Saturday 10.00 - 12.00 and 14.00 - 16.00. At other times by appointment.

A further 1 mile past the church (just after the junction of the road leading to Worth Matravers) is the entrance (on the right) to the Burngate Stone Centre (Tel: 07968557274). The centre was recently opened with the aid of a grant to provide

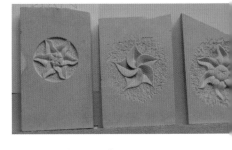

workshops where people can experience the art of masonry, stone carving and letter cutting. The courses vary in length with the shortest taster course for absolute beginners lasting two hours. The centre is named after the field in which it is located. However Reg Saville from the museum points out that the field was actually known as Burnbake, since it was the first field in the village that burnt the stubble at the end of the season to improve the yield for the following year.

DANCING LEDGE

Dancing Ledge is a stretch of flat rock at the edge of the sea, south of Langton Matravers. It derives its name either from the fact that its area is the size of a ballroom dance floor or from the way the waves break over the flat surface. A swimming pool was blasted from the flat rocks for use by children from the local private schools, all of which have long since closed. However the pool is still useable. The flat rock used to be known by the locals as Puffin Bed since puffins nested on it. However they deserted the rock due to the invasion by the local children. The sea is quite deep around here which was of benefit for transporting the stone away.

Dancing Ledge is reached by taking the road (Durnford Drove) 100 yards on the left past St George's church. Continue for ¼ mile – the road becomes a track as it passess between two white posts. There is a small car parking area. The path to Dancing Ledge is about 1 mile long, the last ½ mile being steep with numerous steps.

WORTH MATRAVERS

The village of Worth Matravers derives its name from 'worth' meaning 'enclosure of land' and William Matravers who was one of the original owners of the land and Constable at Corfe Castle. There is evidence of civilisation in the area since 5000 BC. Most of the houses in the village are constructed from Purbeck stone and were originally built between the seventeenth and nineteenth centuries to house quarry workers, fishermen and agricultural workers. Today many of the stone cottages are owned by visitors as second homes. It is a most beautiful village and one can easily spend a full day here, including walks to the Jurassic Coast.

The Square and Compass pub sits on a slope with good views over the village. It was built in 1752 when it was known as the Sloop; the name was changed in 1830. The pub makes its own home-pressed cider. The rooms with their low beamed ceilings are filled with a variety of objects which add to its charm. The pub has a small museum exhibiting fossils and artefacts found in the area. There is usually an expert available who is able to comment on any fossils you may have found. Once a year the pub holds a week-long stone carving festival.

The Square and Compass, Worth Matravers, Swanage, Dorset BH19 3LF Tel: 01929 439229.

Walking into the centre of the village leads to the village green and pond. To the north of the pond are Post Office Cottage and Worth Cottage, the latter now being the local tea shop/restaurant with a restful garden at the rear.

The tea shop is open Monday to Friday, 10.00 - 17.00.

Walking beyond Worth Cottage leads to the village church, dedicated to St Nicholas of Myra, the patron saint of children, sailors, fishermen and pawnbrokers. The church is of Norman origin and was first built around 1100. It was completely restored in 1869. The Norman chancel arch, dating from 1160, immediately strikes you on entering. Almost certainly it was not constructed on the site but brought in from elsewhere, possible from one of the abbeys, such as that at Bindon, which had been destroyed in 1539 during the Dissolution of the Monasteries. In the churchyard are the listed headstones to Elizabeth and Benjamin Jesty. It was known in the eighteenth century that

milkmaids who contracted cowpox from cow's udders were immune to smallpox, which was rife at the time. So when in 1774 smallpox arrived in the locality Benjamin Jesty took his wife and sons to a farm and, using a needle, transferred puss from a cow to their skin by scratching their arms. He was considered by others to be inhuman at the time but neither his wife nor sons subsequently contracted the disease. Twenty years later Edward Jenner began his experiments on vaccinations and he is generally credited with having discovered the process, even though it was first used by Jesty, and Jenner was at pains to point this out.

1 mile beyond St George's church in Langton Matravers and just before the Burngate Stone Centre, is the turning for Worth Matravers. 1 mile further on is the Square and Compass pub. Turn right immediately after the pub and the village car park is a short distance along on the left.

WINSPIT and SEACOMBE

Winspit and Seacombe are both on the South West Coast Path and can be reached on a 3 mile circular tour from Worth Matravers. The area between Winspit and Dancing Ledge was the centre of the Portland stone cliff quarries. Winspit Quarry is the easiest of the old quarry caves to visit. Other caves can be seen on the east side of Winspit valley and the Greater Horseshoe bat uses them for roosting. The 1 mile walk to Winspit is fairly flat but continuing from Winspit to Seacombe and back to Worth is quite difficult with a number of steps to be climbed and may not be suitable for those who are unused to country walking.

London Row Cottages

Stone taken from the Seacombe Quarry was particularly hard. It is thought that the quarry may have been worked as long ago as the seventeenth century.

The well signposted footpath to Winspit starts at the end of the road that passes in front of the London Row Cottages, just south of the village green in Worth Matravers.

Right: View of Winspit from the path on the way to Seacombe

ST ALDHELM'S HEAD

St Aldhelm's Head is referred to as St Alban's Head on the Ordnance Survey maps and by the National Coastwatch Institution However there is no record of St Alban being in the area, whereas Aldhelm was a missionary here and became the first bishop of Sherborne. In addition he was England's first librarian, a scholar and a writer of considerable note. The origins of St Aldhelm's Chapel are not known. One story is that a rich nobleman built it in remembrance of his daughter after he watched her sail away on her honeymoon only to see her drown when the ship foundered. First mention of the chapel was in the middle of the thirteenth century, although it was believed to have been built towards the beginning of the twelfth century; the buttresses were added later. This Norman church is unique; it is 25.5 ft square, its corners face north-south and east-west whereas normally it is a church's walls that do this. Also it has no structural timber and has only one small window on the east

wall. Dominating the interior is a huge rectangular shaped column. The chapel became a ruin in the eighteenth century and underwent

To the east of the lookout is a monument commemorating the development of Radar at RAF Worth Matravers during WWII, which played a major part in the Allies winning the war. A leaflet and booklet detailing the development of Radar at Worth Matravers is available from the staff in the lookout.

A small footpath going from the monument leads to a flight of steps taking visitors part-way down the cliff and giving good views of St Aldhelm's Head and the stone pillars left by earlier quarry workers. This is the southern-most point of the Purbeck Hills and from here, in 1588, would have been seen the sight of Drake fighting the Spanish Armada.

major refurbishment the following century, when the font was added. Services are held in the evenings on the last two Sundays in July and every Sunday in August.

The National Coastwatch lookout had a major refurbishment in 2008/9 thanks to a grant from the Heritage Lottery Fund. The new double-glazing is much appreciated by the team of volunteers who staff the station during the daylight hours of the summer months and who welcome visits from walkers.

Continue through the village of Worth Matravers, past St Nicholas' church, for ¾ mile to the Renscombe carpark. The level, stony road leads after 1½ miles to St Aldhelm's Head, passing St Aldhelm's Head Quarry on the way.

KINGSTON

was designed by George Edmund Street, who also helped with the design of the restoration and enlargement of St Peter's in Bournemouth at the end of the nineteenth century. The church was built as a private family church by the third Lord Eldon as a tribute to his great-grandfather.

No expense was spared in building the church. Most of the Purbeck marble in the church's structure came from local quarries and was worked by local craftsmen. One has to marvel at the workmanship that went into carving the marble columns. The church is considered to be one of the finest Victorian churches in the country. There is a peal of 10 bells (two were added in

Immediately on entering Kingston from the east, attention is drawn to the Scott Arms public house built in 1787. At the time it was known as The New Inn, then in 1807 as the Eldon Arms (after the new owner Lord Eldon) and finally in 1821 the Scott Arms, the family name of the Eldons. From the beer garden at the rear there are good views to Corfe Castle, with Poole Harbour in the background. There is a mounted telescope with which to view the castle in more detail. Kingston village, with its attractive stone cottages, has been the setting for several films, including *Hereward the Wake*, *The Three Musketeers* and *Little Women*, as the framed photos in the Scott Arms testify.

The Scott Arms, West Street, Kingston, Nr Corfe Castle, Wareham, Dorset BH20 5LH. Tel: 01929 480270

Although a small village, Kingston had two churches, both dedicated to St James. The one on the right as you enter Kingston from the east was built by the first Lord Eldon in 1833; it is now a private house. The one a few hundred yards beyond the Scott Arms

2000 to the original eight of 1880) which are also considered to be among the best in the country (to mitigate the sound for the villagers the bell tower has been fitted with wooden baffles!)

The excellent stained glass windows portray figures from the old testament. The organ is interesting in that the bellows and most of the mechanism is housed beneath it in the crypt.

There are plans for the church to be opened every day but for the time being it is necessary to arrange for a warden to be there by phoning the priest Judith Malins, who is also in charge of St George's in Langton Matravers and St Nicholas of Myra in Worth Matravers (01929 422559).

From Worth Matravers, continue on the Corfe Castle Road, adjacent to the Square and Compass. After 1 mile turn left and Kingston is 2 miles further on. If going direct from Langton Matravers then Kingston is 2 miles further on.

The seventeenth century village water pump and cottages close to the church entrance.

CORFE CASTLE

The parish of Corfe Castle shows evidence of human habitation as far back as 6,000BC. The Romans are thought to have been the major force in the area around 50AD and, after they left, the Saxons settled in the area. King Alfred built a wooden castle as defence against the Vikings. In 1090 William II Rufus began work on building a stone castle, which was completed by his heir, Henry I. Henry left no male heir and after his death in the civil war between his daughter Matilda and King Stephen, the castle was held on behalf of Matilda. For the next six hundred years the castle was one of the main castles in England used as home by the monarchs of the time and was said to be King John's favourite castle. It was sold by Queen Elizabeth I and at the time of the Civil War was owned by Sir John Bankes, who supported Charles I. It withstood a six week siege in 1643 by the Parliamentary forces who occupied much of Dorset.

During a second siege in 1646 which lasted two months the Parliamentary forces gained admission to the castle thanks to treachery by one of the castle's officers who let in Parliamentarians disguised as Royalists. Later that year on the order of Parliament, the castle was blown up to ensure it did not return to Royalist hands. The Civil War ended two years later. The demolished castle was then returned to the Bankes family on the reinstatement of the monarchy in 1660. Rather than repair and rebuild the castle, the Bankes family built a new home, Kingston Lacy (page 138), and managed to move many of the treasures from the demolished castle to their new home. Ralph Bankes died in 1981 and the following year the castle passed to the National Trust. In a National Trust survey in December 2008, the castle's majestic ruins were voted the country's fourth-favourite view.

On the south side of the village square is the post office and the Ginger Pop Shop selling almost everything it is possible to sell relating to the works of Enid Blyton. Outside, when the shop is open, is a replica of the Blyton's famous 'wishing chair'. There are over 150 of her books and tapes for purchase, as well as ginger beer, which was the Famous Five's favourite drink and after which the shop is named.

The Castle, the Square, Corfe Castle, Wareham, Dorset BH20 5EZ. Tel: 01929 481294. Open 10.00 - 16.00 in winter and 10.00 - 18.00 in summer.

From Kingston continue to the A351 and then turn left which takes you direct to Corfe Castle.

Enid Blyton was born 11th August 1897 and started writing in 1922, with her first novel published in 1933. She wrote more than 600 books before she died in 1962. It is estimated that more than 600 million of her books have now been sold. She spent three holidays a year in the Isle of Purbeck region and many of her stories are based on places in the area. In her Famous Five books, *Corfe Castle* became Kirrin Castle; *Brownsea Island* became Whispering Island or the Keep Away Island for in those days no visitor was allowed on it; the heath around *Blue Pool* became Mystery Moor; Mr Plod in the Noddy books is said to be based on a Studland policeman. The shop is one of the few places where you can purchase a Golliwog, which frequently featured in the author's stories but was the creation of the American illustrator Florence Upton.

On the west side of the Square is the Bankes Arms Hotel with Station Road alongside leading to the railway station. The hotel used to be known as the Ship and it changed to its present name in the 1960s. The present owner claims that part of it dates back to the middle of the sixteenth century, however most of it dates from

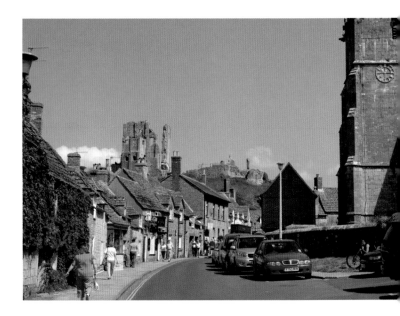

Corfe Model Village

the nineteenth century. The leather front door is from the castle's keep and when viewed from the inside the hinge can be seen which permitted just part of the door to open to see who was asking for admittance. The tables in the dining room to the left when you enter have Purbeck stone tops inlaid with septarian nodules from 160 million years ago. The colours are those of the various minerals that have filtered down over the years into cracks in the rocks and subsequently dried out.

Many of the buildings in the vicinity of the castle are constructed of stone from the demolished castle. Their roofs are Purbeck stone slabs and that on the Bankes Arms Hotel is said to weigh around 100 tons.

Bankes Arms Hotel, East Street, Corfe Castle, Wareham, Dorset BH20 5ED. Tel: 0129 480206.

Opposite the hotel is the parish church of St Edward which can be reached either from East or West Street. The church is dedicated to King Edward and it is said that the King's body was taken to the site on which the church now stands, after he had been murdered by his step-mother. A large church was built on the site in the thirteenth century but it fell into a state of disrepair at the end of the eighteenth century. All but the tower was demolished in 1859 when a new church was built.

On the west side of West Street, 100 yards from the Square, is the Corfe Castle Model Village, set in an acre of landscaped gardens. Recreated is the village of Corfe Castle as it was believed to have been in 1646.

The Model Village, the Square, Corfe Castle, Dorset BH20 5EZ. Tel: 0129 481234 Open daily during the summer from 10.00 - 17.00.

Fox Inn

Shortly beyond is the Fox Inn, said to be the oldest pub in the village dating from 1568.

The upstairs part of the building opposite the Fox Inn is the smallest Town Hall in the country, while the downstairs is a museum and has many items of interest, although it is quite small.

The Swanage Railway train stops at Corfe Castle. The A351 from Swanage or Wareham passes through the centre of the village. From Studland, keep on the B3351, for 8 miles to the A351. The castle is 300 yards to the left. The National Trust car park and Castle View Visitor Centre which explores the lives of the many past residents of the castle are 100 yards to the right. The road to Church Knowle and Tyneham is directly ahead.

Town Hall

CHURCH KNOWLE

The Trust rescues and re-homes more than 800 animals per year. At any one time there can be several hundred animals on the 35 acre site. However the sanctuary is built for the animals and not for humans so the animals are not always easy to spot and may be in the distance. There is a large, and very pleasant, garden of remembrance for the animals. It is the largest and oldest rescue centre in Dorset.

"This is Pumpkin, a 9 year old Vietnamese pot belly pig who needs a home. She is very friendly and enjoys having her belly scratched."

The village of Church Knowle was known as 'Cnolle' (i.e. top of a hill) in Saxon times and there is thought to have been a church here from that time. In fact the only priest in Purbeck mentioned in the Domesday Book was the one associated with Cnolle and this is thought to be how the village got its name. However another suggestion is that the name comes from the fact that the village church is built on a round burial mound or 'knoll'. The church of St Peter dates from the thirteenth century with major alterations made to it in the early part of the nineteenth century.

Margaret Green died on Christmas Eve 2009 aged 94 but she had made sure that all the horses had received their special treat of Christmas Day Carrots. She started the Sanctuary in 1965 and had lived on it for the next five years before moving home into the village of Church Knowle. She remained very active in the sanctuary until 2000 when she 'retired'.

It is a pleasant village with thatched stone cottages. 300 yards past the church is the New Inn; fish meals are their speciality but you may need to book in the summer period.

The Margaret Green Animal Sanctuary is 150 yards on the left past the New Inn. There are a number of Margaret Green Animal Sanctuaries in the area but this is the only one open to visitors. The sanctuary has all types of animals, other than dogs. The main aim of the trust is to care for all unwanted or injured animals until their natural death or until they can be found a suitable home.

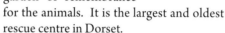
Margaret Green Foundation Trust Animal Sanctuary, Church Knowle, Wareham, Dorset BH20 5NQ. Tel: 01929 480474 Free Admission. Open: Daily 10.00 - 16.00.

Leave Corfe Castle on the A351 to Wareham; the road to Church Knowle is ¼ mile on the left, at the foot of the castle. If coming direct from the ferry then keep on the B3351, for 8 miles to the A351. (There is a viewing point on the right after 5 miles.) Turn right and immediately left. The church at Church Knowle is 1½ miles on the right. Parking is a further hundred yards on the left.

KIMMERIDGE BAY

Kimmeridge is a village with around 100 residents. To the north, just before the car park, is the small village church of St Nicholas. Parts of it date from Norman times but the majority from 1872 when it underwent a major refurbishment. There are a number of memorials to the Clavell family, who owned much of the land in the area. Near the west wall of the churchyard is a line of gravestones in memory of the Kimmeridge coastguards.

Passing the Clavell Farm House Café leads to a number of attractive, thatched cottages, with beautiful gardens. The road continues through the village for another ¾ mile (there is a toll just beyond the village). From the cliff-top car park, an easy walk leads down to the pebbled beach.

Kimmeridge Bay has a thin seam of Blackstone (a shaly bituminous stone) often referred to as 'Kimmeridge Coal' and in the past was used as fuel, albeit a rather smelly one. It has been worked since prehistoric times and the Romans used it to make large quantities of jewellery.

A number of fossils have been found in the Bay and, although visitors may remove any found laying on the surface, hammering for them is forbidden. The cliff formation here is very interesting. Unusually there are double low tides which makes the area ideal for visitors to paddle and explore the many ledges and pools.

By driving directly into the area sign posted for boats, you come to the headquarters of the Purbeck Marine Wildlife Reserve. The reserve, established in 1978, is the longest established marine nature reserve in the UK, extending over eight miles along the Purbeck coast. The headquarters in an old fisherman's hut has several fish tanks housing local fish and other marine life. An underwater camera relays pictures to the centre from the bay. The area is a common launching spot for diving boats, with many wrecks, reefs and fossils in the area. During the summer months there is a recognised snorkelling trail through the

shallow waters and a waterproof guide is available from the centre. The steps signposted to Chapman's Pool lead to Clavell Tower from where there are good views of the bay.

The 40 ft folly known as Clavel Tower was built as a summer house in 1830 and is now Grade II listed. The tower, named after the Clavell family, was built by the local vicar John Clavell. In 2006, and at a cost of around £1million, it was moved 85ft inland to save it from the eroding cliff edge. It took two years to move the 16,272 bricks and the process has been recognised as one of the world's finest architectural achievements. It was restored at the same time and is now available for short lets via the Landmark Trust. It was referred to in novels by both Thomas Hardy and P. D. James and indeed Thomas Hardy is said to have done some of his courting in the tower.

To the west of Kimmeridge Bay is BP's 1959 'nodding donkey' extracting 100 barrels of oil a day from 1,000 feet below the surface.

Clavel Tower

Purbeck Marine Wildlife Reserve, Fine Foundation Marine Centre, Kimmeridge Bay, Wareham, BH20 5PF. Tel: 01929 481044. Open: Tuesday - Sunday, Easter to October, from 10.00 - 17.00.

From the Animal Sanctuary in Church Knowle continue for 1½ miles and then turn left - the road leads direct to Kimmeridge. There is a car park adjacent to Clavell's Restaurant.

STEEPLE

The village of Steeple is referred to in the Domesday book as 'Stiple', meaning 'steep place'. The point of note in the village is the church of St Michael and All Angels and its connection with America; the church is regularly visited by Americans. On the outside of the church, above the doorway on the north face, is carved a coat of arms. There are similar flags on the right of the porch as you enter and on the ceiling. In two of the quarters of the flag can be seen three Stars and two Stripes (or three 'Mullets' and two 'Bars' as they are correctly known). It is dated 1616 and is the coat of arms resulting from the marriage of Edmund Lawrence and Agnes de Wessington in 1390. Their descendants moved to Steeple in 1540. Another branch of the family moved to America in 1657 and one of their descendents, George Washington, became the first President of the United States. The stars and stripes flag derives from this connection. The other point of significance in the church is the 1858 barrel organ which was in regular use until 1890. It was fully restored 100 years later and is believed to be the only such organ in existence. It has three barrels, each with 12 hymns.

From Church Knowle, the turning for Steeple Church is ¼ mile after the turning for Kimmeridge; the church is then 300 yards on the right.

THE GHOST VILLAGE OF TYNEHAM

There had been populations in the area of Tyneham since the Iron Age. The Romans occupied the area and the nearby costal village of Worbarrow was used extensively by both fishermen and smugglers. It was mentioned in the Domesday Book under the name of Tigeham. However in November 1943, during the Second World War, the 250 villagers were told that they had to leave as the area was required by the Army. They were expecting to move back at the end of the war but this never happened and in 1948 the Army purchased, by means of a compulsory purchase order, the village of around 100 buildings and the surrounding land. Since then there have been several attempts to return the village to the original owners but for a variety of reasons this has not happened. The village is now in a serious derelict state with many buildings in ruins and some too dangerous to enter and are cordoned off. Post Office Row (shown above) was the main street in the village.

In 1977 the Army made some of the buildings in the village safe and leased St Mary's church for use as a museum. However the church's organ, bell and pulpit that had been removed at the time of

evacuation for safe keeping have never been returned. (The church was built in the thirteenth century and had a major refurbishment in the middle of the eighteenth century).

When the villagers left in 1943 they were told that they would be able to return after the war and they pinned to the door of the church a hand-written notice asking people to treat the village kindly.

The village had been sufficiently large to have its own, single roomed school which was for village children whatever their age, although the school closed in 1932. This too has been repaired and turned into a museum and looks much as it would have done when last used.

Walking south out of the village beyond the car park leads to the ruins of Tyneham Farm.

Please treat the church and houses with care; we have given up our homes where many of us lived for generations to help win the war to keep men free. We shall return one day and thank you for treating the village kindly.

To find out whether the Army's gunnery range is open to the public phone 01929 404819. It is normally open every weekend and every day during the summer season and over Christmas.

Tyneham lies within the Army's gunnery range. When the range is open, then the church and school are open from 10.00 - 16.00.

From Church Knowle, continue for a further ¾ mile past the turn off to Steeple Church and then turn left. ¼ mile further on fork left and Tyneham is 1½ miles further on.

*The barn for storing grain was mounted on mushroom
shaped stones to prevent rodents gaining access to it*

The village pond was probably a cobbled ford and the main approach to the farm

Below: *The stables*

Below: *Restored cart*

WORBARROW BAY

The secluded Worbarrow Bay is arguably the most beautiful part of the Dorset coast. It is only open to the public when the Army are not using the firing range, which generally means it is only open at weekends.

On the east of the bay is the conical hill of Worbarrow Tout, (opposite), which derives its name from the old English word meaning 'look-out hill'. The markings on the hill assist tank ranging. On the east of Worbarrrow Tout is Pondfield Cove, still with the concrete blocks which were built to prevent the landing of enemy tanks during the war. The bay further east is Brandy Bay, so named because of the smuggling carried on there.

Towards the end of the path leading to the bay are the remains of a Tett Turret. The turrets were designed for shielding solders during an invasion and would hold a single machine-gunner as illustrated in the near-by information panel. The base was sunk into the ground, whilst the top could revolve.

On leaving Tyneham Farm, continue on the footpath directly ahead. It is a ¾ mile level walk, even the paths down to the beach are not too steep.

LULWORTH CASTLE

Lulworth Castle was built in 1610 as a hunting lodge to host hunting parties for the King. The castle and estates were purchased by the Weld family in 1641 and have been owned by the family ever since. Unfortunately the interior of the castle was completed gutted by a fire that lasted three days in August 1929 and for the next 70 years the castle remained empty until it was opened to the public in 1998 following restoration by English Heritage. Today a large metal spiral staircase allows you to pass up the building through the empty flours to the battlements, from where there are good views over the surrounding countryside. In the basement are a number of interesting exhibits.

To the south of the castle, although not in the estate itself, is the

parish church of St Andrew whose records date from 1561 although most of the church dates from around the 1860s. At one time the church was in the centre of the village but the houses were demolished and rebuilt outside of the Lulworth Castle estate.

To the north of the castle is St Mary's church. It was the first free-standing Roman Catholic church to be built after the Reformation. The inside is beautiful and is still used for mass.

The Lulworth estate also has an animal farm and adventure play area.

Lulworth Castle, East Lulworth, Wareham, Dorset BH20 5QS. Tel: 0845 4501054. Open 10.30 - 18.00 (10.30 -16.00 in winter) closed on Saturdays.

Leave Wareham on the A352 towards Dorchester. After 1¼ miles turn left on the B3070. After 4 miles the road bears right in front of the Weld Arms; the castle entrance is immediately on the right. There are clear directions from Tyneham if the roads are open.

DURDLE DOOR

Durdle Door is one of the country's most recognisable and photographed sights. It is a limestone promontory jutting into the sea and the arch has been cut through by the sea over millions of years. UNESCO is working to save the arch from further erosion. This area of the coastline is owned by the Lulworth estate who are responsible for maintaining it, together with the footpaths. The Government is considering plans to take control of all the coastline so as to make a well-cared for coastal path in time for the 2012 Olympics to be held at Weymouth and Portland. There are concerns as to whether the necessary funding to do this, estimated at around £30,000 per mile of coastline, will be found.

To the west of Durdle Door is Man o'War Bay which can be clearly seen on the walk down to Durdle Door. The walk to it from the cliff car park is long and steep.

On leaving Lulworth Castle turn right and after 1½ miles turn left at the T-junction. Continue through West Lulworth village for another mile and then turn right. Turn left after ¾ mile. The car park is ½ mile further on, through the Holiday Park.

LULWORTH COVE

The Lulworth Heritage Centre has a number of displays showing the natural history of the area and explaining how the various rock formations have developed over the past few million years. A recent addition to the centre is the displays outlining the Social History of the Stone, Iron and Bronze Ages. The shop attached to the centre has a variety of rocks and fossils for sale.

Lulworth Heritage Centre, Main Road, West Lulworth, Wareham, Dorset BH20 5QS. Tel: 01929 400587. Open daily: 10.00 - 18.00 Summer; 10.00 - 16.00 Winter.

Walking beyond the Lulworth Cove Inn leads to the Little Shop (selling a variety of clothes and either items), Cove Fish (selling fresh fish) and then the cove.

The cove was formed when the sea breached the outer rocks around 10,000 years ago and then eroded the softer rock and clay beyond. The shell-shaped nature of the cove can best be appreciated from the air, although walking up one of the paths to the west gives visitors a good view of it, as well as of West Lulworth. A short distance further along, the path overlooks Stair Hole where the sea has breached the outer cliff and begun eroding the softer clays. Here can be seen one of the finest examples of limestone folding in the world. This 'Lulworth Crumple' as it is known, has been formed by the earth's crust moving and forcing the rocks up through 90°.

Around 200 million years ago, during the Jurassic period, a tropical forest of giant cypresses existed in the area. The trees were later flooded by the sea and algae formed round the

Fossil Forest

base of the tree trunks to form doughnut shaped burrs. The area has what is said to be the most complete fossil record of any Jurassic forest in the world. To reach the Fossil Forest walk eastward along the pebbled beach of Lulworth Cove until you reach the wooden steps. Turn right at the top of the steps and follow the signs to the Fossil Forest. The forest is in the Army's firing range and the gate leading to the forest is only open when the range is open. The walk takes about 1 - 1½ hours, including the slow walk across the pebbles.

The rock formation in the forest is of striking appearance.

Boat trips leave from the cove during the summer to give visitors a trip round the area.

From Durdle Door, return to the main road and turn right. Lulworth Cove is ¼ mile further on.

'Lulworth Crumple'

BLUE POOL

Blue Pool is in the midst of 25 acres of heath and woodland, which has a number of marked paths through it. The area has been designated as a Site of Special Scientific Interest due to the many rare plants and animals in the area. The water in the pool constantly changes colour as the light is refracted at different angles from the millions of tiny clay particles that are suspended in the water. One moment it can be shades of green and the next turquoise. Top

quality clay had been extracted from the pit since the seventeenth century and was used by such companies as Wedgwood, Minton and Royal Worcester, indeed the clay was regarded as the best in the country. It was open cast clay mining, whereby the workers would simply fill their wheelbarrows with the clay and wheel it out of the pit or, when possible, use a donkey to transport it. When the pit became uneconomic for clay extraction, the pumps removing the water from the pit were turned off and the pool as you see it today started to be formed. The pool was opened to the public for the first time in 1935. There are no streams feeding the pool so all the water is rainwater and fishes are unable to live in it. Steps lead down to the water's edge.

On the north side of the pool is a museum which explains the history of clay mining in the area, with examples of products made from the clay; in particular there is a good collection of clay pipes. A shop and tea room serve light lunches.

The Blue Pool, Furzebrook, Nr Wareham, Dorset BH20 5AT. Tel: 01929 551408. Open: March - November 09.30-17.00.

Leave Corfe Castle, travelling north on the A351, and continue for 3 miles to the roundabout; take the first exit. After 1¼ miles turn left and parking is 200 yards further on.

WAREHAM

There is evidence of human habitation in the Wareham area more than 3,500 years ago. During the Roman occupation in the first century, Wareham was the centre for crossing the Rivers Piddle and Frome. They laid out the town with one road going north-south and the other east-west and the layout continues to the present time. By the eighth century the town was part of the Saxon Kingdom of Wessex, constantly under attack from the sea route by pirates and Vikings. To defend themselves the town was fortified but nevertheless was overrun by the Vikings in 876 when attacked landward from the north rather than, as expected, seaward from the south. The following year King Alfred recaptured Wareham and in a sea battle the Vikings lost around 120 ships in Swanage Bay. King Alfred then further fortified the town and it entered a period of prosperity. By the time of King Athelstan (King Alfred's grandson and the first King of all England) Wareham was at the height of its prosperity. After the Norman Conquest the town's fortification was increased by the building of stone walls and also bridges over the Rivers Piddle and Frome. The town now started to lose its prosperity. The building of Wareham Castle only added to the decline since the town was now involved in many years of civil war (1135 –54) as King Stephen and Queen Matilda fought for the throne and the town was captured first by one and then the other. Traders left for a more peaceful life in Hamworthy. The decline continued when in 1250 Poole obtained its first charter as a port and the new larger ships were able to use Poole Harbour when they could not reach Wareham Quay. The last Monarch to use Wareham Castle was Edward I (1272 - 1307). By the sixteenth century it was derelict although when the castle was actually demolished is not known. There is no mention of Wareham as a port after 1350 and its decline as a major town in England was now almost complete. During the Civil War, Wareham supported the Royalists but the town was captured and recaptured several times by both Royalist and Parliamentarians.

This former great settlement once had a castle, two royal mints and seven churches (sadly only three remain and only one of these, namely Lady St Mary, is still used for worship). Kings were buried here, namely Bertic, King of the West Saxons in the year 800 and King Edward the Martyr in 978. The Great Fire on 25 July 1762 destroyed two thirds of the town but there still remains much to be appreciated in Wareham and its surrounding areas.

POOLE TO WAREHAM BY RIVER

During the summer holiday season boats tours go to Wareham up the River Frome from Poole Quay. At other times it is possible to hire a yacht for the 1 to 1½ hour trip. However the river is very shallow towards Wareham and at low tides there are places where the depth of the river is zero due to sand and mud banks. At the time the author went, although it was almost a high tide, the yacht was unable to make it. The locals said that the tide was 'funny' and that it was clearly falling, although by all accounts it should have been rising. Ours was not the only boat unable to make it as there was a queue of others waiting for an opportunity to progress. However it was possible to leave the yacht and walk the remaining short distance to Wareham along the river-side path.

The boat trip leaves Poole Quay and travels past Hamworthy with its large shipping berths, the listed boat house and then Rockley Park (page 42). Through the several boats moored you are likely to see

the Royal Marines training – they are the only ones permitted to exceed the 4 knots per hour speed limit in the main part of the harbour. At the entrance to the river is a speed restriction sign and the reeds become noticeably narrower and the progression of the boat slows down as the depth of the river varies. It is hard to imagine that many years ago this was the main route by which the Vikings invaded Wessex in their longboats. Various birds can be heard and with luck a sika deer seen On reaching Wareham, there is an excellent view of Lady St Mary church across the river.

Cruises, including those round the harbour, up to Wareham, to Brownsea Island, along the Jurassic Coast, to the Isle of Wight, Beaulieu River and bird-watching, are available from Greenslade Pleasure Boats (01202 631828), Brownsea Island Ferries (01929 462383), Dorset Cruises (0845 4684640). For sailing boat hire with crew try Puffin Charters (01202 667050).

POOLE TO WAREHAM BY ROAD

The most enjoyable way to Wareham by road is to cross to Studland using the chain ferry (page 60) and follow the route into Swanage and then join the A351 to Corfe Castle and directly to Wareham. 3.5 miles after joining the A351 is the Purbeck Vineyard. The vineyard was started in 2000 and has over 3000 vines and several varieties, including Purbeck Chardonnay. The vineyard is open to the public by arrangement throughout the year and a self-guided tour

Purbeck Vineyard, Corfe Castle, Dorset BH20 5HU Tel: 01929 481 525.

leaflet is available. The vineyard also arranges organised tours and tasting sessions. Needless to say they have their wines for sale, although several have a long waiting list. The vineyard has a four star guest accommodation and restaurant.

If you want to miss out Swanage and Corfe, then keep on the B3351 from the chain ferry for eight miles to the A 351. (There is a viewing point on the right after five miles). Turn right and the road leads direct to Wareham.

Wareham can also be approached from the north. Join the A35 Dorchester Road and about four miles west of Poole take the A351 road to Wareham (first exit on the roundabout). 3½ miles further on take the first left at the roundabout signposted to the Town Centre. A few hundred yards further on turn left into Dollin's Lane and park in one of the three car parks.

WAREHAM TOWN TRAIL

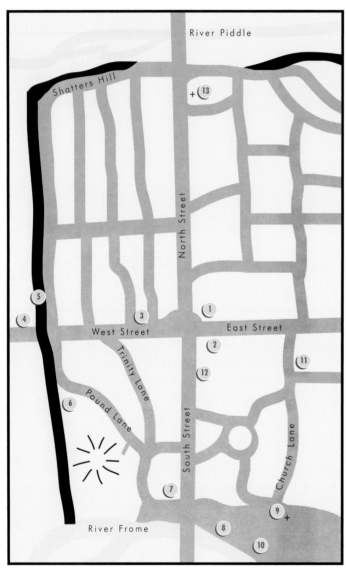

Map for Wareham Town Trail - Trinity Lane follows the route of the outer bailey and Pound Lane of the inner bailey.

1. Exiting from the town's car park leads to the corner of North and East Streets where the Town Hall is located. The original building on the site was a church which was later used as a Town Hall, school and then gaol. It was rebuilt for its present use as a Town Hall in 1870. Part of the lower floor is given over to the small but interesting **Wareham Town Museum.** The museum resulted from a private collection owned by a former mayor of Wareham, Harry Broughton. The council purchased the collection and moved it to its present site. The museum has a collection showing the history of Wareham dating back through many centuries and a collection of pottery made during the Roman period. Part of the museum is dedicated to T. E. Lawrence (Lawrence of Arabia), who was a regular visitor to the town after he purchased **Clouds Hill Cottage.**

Wareham Town Museum, East Street, Wareham, Dorset BH20 4NN Tel: 01929 553448 Open: April to October , Monday - Saturday 10.00 - 16.00. Free admission.

2. Opposite the museum on East Street are the old **Almshouses** (now converted into apartments) dating from 1741. The bell tower was moved to the Almshouses from the Town Hall when the Town Hall was rebuilt in 1870.

3. Across the square and along West Street is the **Rex Cinema**. The building, built in 1889, was originally the Oddfellows Hall. It first became a cinema in 1920 when it opened as the Empire Theatre and is one of the oldest cinemas in the country and still has double seats in the back row for courting couples! The cinema is the main venue for the Purbeck Film Festival, held every October.

4. Just beyond the Rex Cinema are the Town's earthen walls and a few hundred yards beyond is another row of **Almshouses**. These were built in 1908 from an endowment set up by a Mr Streches in 1418.

5. The **earthen walls** are believed to date from the time of the Saxons in the ninth century. They are of national importance and have Scheduled Ancient Monument status. The walls defended the town on three sides, with the River Frome defending the fourth side. You can walk along the top of most of the walls. A manor house has been built on top of the West Wall, just before the Almshouses.

6. Walking west down Pound Lane, opposite the walls brings you to the **Old Brewery,** now converted into residential properties.

7. At the end of Pound Lane and then right along South Street leads to Holy Trinity church, dating from the fourteenth Century. The original Saxon church on the site had been dedicated to St Andrew but was severely damaged by fire in 1137, along with much of the town. The new church, now dedicated to the Holy Trinity, was itself severely destroyed by fire in 1762, again with much of the town. Up until then it had been Wareham's main church but this distinction then passed to the Lady St Mary church. It was rebuilt but by 1830 had fallen into disuse. After various uses the church is now the town's **Information and Heritage Centre.**

Purbeck Information & Heritage Centre, Holy Trinity church, South Street, Wareham, Dorset BH20 4LU. Open 09.30 - 17.00. Tel: 01929 552740.

8. Continuing along South Street, brings you to the River Frome and *the Quay*. This was once the hub of Wareham where the ships unloaded. Today tourist boats cruise along the River Frome, while food and drinks are available at the Old Granary which was once a warehouse. Also on the Quay are the public toilets with, on the outside, a tiled map of old Wareham and the Quay Inn.

Boats can be hired from the west side of the bridge. Wareham Boat Hire, Abbots Quay, Wareham BH20 4LW. Tel 01929 550688.

9. Leaving the Quay through the north-east corner leads to the *Lady St Mary's church* (page 110).

10. Between the church and the river is the **Priory Hotel.** The building dates from the sixteenth century. A priory is believed to have existed on the site as early as the eighth century and was probably set up by St Aldhelm. The hotel has leaflets outlining its bloody history over the years. It ceased to be a priory in 1536 after King Henry VIII's dissolution of the monasteries. The grounds are beautiful and well worth a visit.

The Priory Hotel, Church Green, Wareham, Dorset BH20 4ND. Tel: 01929 551666.

11. Walking north up Church Lane brings you, on the right, to the *Congregational Church.* Much of the building dates from the year of the Great Fire in 1762 when the original building was destroyed.

12. Continuing along Church Lane and turning left along East Street brings you back to the Wareham Museum. 100 yards down South Street on the left is the *Manor House* dating from 1712 and still with its original flat roof.

13. Along North Street are a number of interesting buildings, including the Black Bear Hotel dating from 1770, with a life size statue of a bear on the porch roof. While at the end of North Street is **St Martin's church**, one of the most complete Saxon churches in England with the nave and chancel dating from before the Norman Conquest. It is a 'must see' for anyone who has any interest in ancient churches. The tower, the lower part of which is the porch and door, dates from the first part of the sixteenth century although the top was rebuilt at the start of the eighteenth century. For 200 years the church was hardly used and for 100 of them it was bricked up until refurbished and rededicated in 1936. Above the chancel arch is an eighteenth century fresco with Queen Anne's coat of arms and the ten commandments. Some of the wall paintings date from the twelfth century. There is also a life size effigy of Lawrence of Arabia in Arabic dress and a number of most interesting scrap books relating to him. The church is usually open Monday to Saturday from Easter to October but if not the key can be obtained from the church warden at AF Joy Outfitters, 35 North Street.

About 50 yards past St Martin's church, on the left, is Shatters Hill which passes alongside the village walls and reveals the true extent of them The road probably derives its name from the shattering of the nearby town's gates by the Parliamentarians. There is a car park a short way along. It was on these walls in 1214 that King John had Peter of Pomfret hanged and quarterd. The poor man had foretold that King John would be dead by the time of the next Ascension Day. On hearing this the King had Peter imprisoned in Corfe Castle until Ascension Day came when he was dragged by horse around Wareham before being hanged in front of all the townsfolk. Shakespeare refers to the incident in Act IV, Scene I of *King John*.

> The town has more than 200 buildings of significant architectural interest and a detailed guide can be obtained from the Information Centre.

A tiled map of old Wareham can be found on the Quay

LADY ST MARY CHURCH

There was a church on the site from the seventh century when it was one of the most important churches in Europe. It was demolished in 1840, to be replaced by the present church two years later.

King Edward inherited the throne at the age of 13. He was murdered in Corfe Castle in 978 and the 17 year old King was initially buried in the place where the church's St Edward's chapel now is. A year later his body was reburied in the abbey at Shaftesbury. The Chapel itself dates from about 1100.

The font, also dating from around 1100, is made from lead and is one of the finest of the 30 or so such fonts in the country. It is also unique in that it is the only one that is hexagonal. The figures around the bowl are of the 12 apostles.

The heating system was installed in 1882. Hot water flows through square pipes with chevron markings. The pipes rest directly onto the tiled floor in a single ring-main round each of the pew islands, with the height of the pew raised so as to be level with the pipes.

The church is open from 11.00 - 17.00 in summer and 11.00 - 15.00 in winter.

ARNE

The area of Arne protrudes into Poole Harbour. The word 'Arne' derives from an Anglo-Saxon word meaning 'dwelling' or 'house'. Today the area is almost uninhabited but in the past this was not the case and in fact had been inhabited for thousands of years. In more recent times it was the workers extracting clay for the pottery industry who lived here. The area was evacuated during the Second World War and fires were lit to try to deceive the German bombers into bombing this area rather than the cordite factories several miles to the north. Many of the ponds in the area are the craters formed by bombs dropped during the war. All that remains in the area now are its church, a few houses, a farm, the toy museum and of course the birds, the flora and the fauna

Much of the land is owned and managed by the RSPB and the area, known as the Arne Nature Reserve, is one of the most important bird sanctuaries in the country with over 200 different species as well as around 500 types of flowering plants. Among the birds that can be seen are ospreys when migrating back to Africa, kestrels and buzzards. The society is attempting to encourage the ospreys to breed in the area by placing life-sized polystyrene ospreys in artificial eyries. It is in fact the RSPB's flagship heathland reserve. Although much of the sanctuary is not open to the general public, there are a number of nature trails and hides.

Arne Nature Reserve, Arne Road, Arne, Wareham, BH20 5BJ. Tel 01929 553360. Open: Daily 09.00 - 17.00.

Leave Wareham by the south bridge and ½ mile further on just pass the Texaco garage and the Kings Arms is a narrow road on the left, which leads, after 3½ miles, direct to Arne.

The toy museum is directly opposite the car park. It was formed in 1986 on a 1½ acre site. The collection consists of thousands of toys dating back to 1850. There are more than 40 end-of-pier amusements machines, including 'What the Butler Saw', and all are in working order. A place to wallow in nostalgia.

Arne Toy Museum, Arne House, Arne, Nr Wareham, Dorset BH20 5BJ. Tel 01929 552018. Open: April to September, Tuesday - Sunday 11.00 - 17.00.

Walking along the road between the museum and car park brings you shortly to the church of St Nicholas of Myra which has Saxon origins. It was built by monks around 1220 AD on the orders of the daughter of King Alfred. The church still has its original lancet windows from which there are good views to the coast. The church is open daily, with services held at 10.30 or 11.15 on the 1st and 3rd Sundays of each month. (Tel: 01929 550905).

A short distance past the farm on the left is a path that leads to the marshes and harbour, while the one to the right leads to the beach at Shipstall Point. The whole area is, as you would expect, very quiet and peaceful.

MONKEY WORLD

The Monkey World Rescue Centre was originally established to house abused chimpanzees from Spanish beaches where they had been used as photographic props. In almost all cases their teeth had been removed so that they could not bite tourists. Now animals are brought to the sanctuary from all over the world.

The centre was set up in 1987 by Jim Cronin. He was awarded the MBE in 2006 for his conservation work but he died of cancer in 2007 before he could collect the honour. In the heart of the park is a memorial to him in the form of a life-size bronze sculpture with Charlie, one of the first chimpanzees he saved. Charlie arrived in 1989 with a broken jaw, missing teeth, machete scars, cataracts and a broken foot. He is still alive and enjoying life with 14 other chimpanzees. Since Jim's death, his wife Alison has carried on the work.

There are over 240 primates of 15 different species in the 65 acre site. Chimpanzees, orang-utans, gibbons (including the endangered Golden-Checked gibbon), lemurs and monkeys. They are kept in large social groups, similar to their life in the wild. Most of the females are on birth control so there will remain space for other rescued creatures, although the sanctuary also takes part in the breeding of endangered species. The centre has its own hospital and operating theatre and most of the staff are experts in the rehabilitation and wellbeing of the primates. It has the largest chimpanzee colony outside of Africa. The sanctuary is the only one in the world that has an increasing number of woolly monkeys, which is an endangered species.

The park works with governments around the world to help in the elimination of the illegal smuggling of animals from their natural habitats in Africa. It is estimated that for every one primate captured by poachers, up to another ten are killed as the parents attempt to protect their young. A captured primate frequently has a life span of only five years before it is killed because it has become uncontrollable. The largest single group of animals to join the centre were 88 capuchin monkeys saved from a laboratory in Santiago, Chile where most of them had been kept in solitary cages for up to 20 years.

Monkey World has won national and international awards for its work. It has been voted best family attraction in the country and is frequently featured on television.

There is a small pets corner, a large children's play area, a shop and a cafeteria. There are half-hourly talks relating to the different primates and they are worth attending . There is also the opportunity to adopt one of the primates.

Monkey World, Longthorns, Wareham, BH20 6HH Tel: 01929 462537. Open: Daily from 10.00 - 18.00 or 10.00 - 17.00 in winter.

From Wareham Museum travel along West Street with the Rex Cinema on your right. ½ mile further on cross the roundabout on to the A352 Dorchester Road. Continue for 4 miles to the next roundabout and turn right. Monkey world is 1 mile further along on the right.

From Bournemouth, join the A35 Dorchester Road and about 4 miles west of Poole take the A351 to Wareham. 3½ miles further on take the second exit at the roundabout and then turn right at the next roundabout on to the A352 Dorchester Road. Continue for 4 miles to the next roundabout and turn right. Monkey World is 1mile further along on the right.

TANK MUSEUM

The Bovington Army Training Camp was established in 1916 and it was here that the British tanks returned after the First World War and where they were then used for training. Future tanks also returned here and the idea of having a Tank Museum was proposed by Rudyard Kipling in 1923. It was not until 1947 that such a museum opened to the paying public. Bovington is now home to the world's greatest collection of tanks. It has examples from the first tank ever built, which is still in working order, to the modern day Challenger II. There is the massive Tiger I (No 131) weighing almost 70 tons and which spearheaded Nazi Germany's World War II efforts. This is probably the most famous of the WWII tanks, with 1354 of them having been built. It was by far the largest

tank at the time and much feared by the allies with its almost impenetrable armour and fearsome 88mm gun. Due to their enormous thirst for fuel they were often used in a static defence role. Now only six of them remain of which the Tank Museum has the only one in working order; it was acquired by the museum in 1951. It was in fact the first one to be captured intact by the allies as the Germans were under instructions to destroy them rather than to allow them to fall into Allied hands. Other tanks include more recently captured Iraqi machines. In all, there are over 200 tanks as well as another 100 other military vehicles dating from 1909 from 26 countries; all are in working order.

The museum tells the story of the development of the tank to the

There are over 300 names so far inscribed on it.

The museum recently had a £16m development with the help of funding from the Heritage Lottery Fund. The new 50,000 sq ft display hall houses 30 tanks and many of them had not been moved for at least 25 years prior to moving to their new home. Visitors can hear the voices of those who actually fought in them and, for an additional fee, ride in or drive one themselves, although this may need to be pre-booked.

present day. The tank is a British invention and the Army wanted to surprise the Germans with their new weapon. So rather than call it a 'landship' from which the Germans might have deduced what was being planned, they chose the name 'tank'.

As you first enter the museum you have an opportunity to experience a recruiting office for the First World War, a walk through what would have been mud-filled trenches and see inside Command Headquarters. It was to overcome the impasse resulting from the trenches that resulted in the tank being invented and the wider the Germans made their trenches the longer the British made their tanks

In 2008 an eight-foot high, Portland stone memorial was erected to those members of the Household Cavalry and the Royal Armoured Corps who have been killed on active service since 1945.

There are displays of small arms, medals, anti-tank guns, experimental designs and a collection in honour of T.E. Lawrence who served in the Tank Corps at Bovington using the assumed name of Private Shaw. There is also the largest collection of armoured warfare publications in the world, including diaries, transcripts and over 250,000 photographs. This collection is open daily from 10.00-16.00 but an appointment is required to see it and there is an additional fee to be paid. The Tank Museum is still part of the country's main army camp for training members of the armed forces in tank warfare. The RAC Roll of Honour lists the names of every RAC soldier killed since the formation of the corps in April 1939.

There is almost too much to take in on a single visit. Fortunately the tickets are valid for as many visits as you want within a year. There are 30 minute tank action displays from Monday to Friday at 1300 during the school holiday period. The amenities include a licensed restaurant.

Tank Museum, Bovington, Wool, Dorset BH20 6JG Tel: 01929 405096. Open: Daily from 10.00 - 17.00.

On leaving Monkey World, turn left retuning the way you came. The road to the Tank Museum is ½ mile along on the right, with the entrance a further ¾ mile further along on the right.
On leaving the Tank Museum, turn right and 1¼ miles on the right is a viewing area for watching the tanks going to and from their training ground.

CLOUDS HILL COTTAGE

The isolated Clouds Hill Cottage is a short distance from the Bovington Army Training Camp. It was first rented by Thomas Edward Lawrence (Lawrence of Arabia) in 1923 using the name Aircraftsman Shaw so as to keep his anonymity after his return from North Africa. He purchased the cottage two years later and returned there in 1935 after he left the RAF. Whilst staying there he had a motor bike accident which caused his death and he died in the Bovington Camp Hospital. His brother inherited the cottage and gave it to the National Trust and it remains much as it was when Lawrence lived there. Lawrence rarely slept at the cottage whilst he was based at Bovington Camp but spent evenings there reading and listening to music. He kept a sleeping bag for his visitors, as well as keeping one for himself. The visitor's bag was stolen shortly after the release of the film *Lawrence of Arabia* but was returned anonymously from Belgium in 2001. It is thought that visitors who used the sleeping bag included George Bernard Shaw, E. M. Forster and Robert Graves. There is a flight of stairs directly opposite the front door leading to the bedroom on the right and his music room on the left. Downstairs to the right is the bathroom (there is no WC - he used one in the garden). On the left is the living room with a large leather-covered double bed and a display of books and photos depicting his life. The garage now houses an exhibition of Lawrence's life but would have contained his motorbikes.

Clouds Hill, Wareham, Dorset BH20 7NQ. Tel: 01929 405616. Open: March to October on Thursday, Friday, Saturday and Sunday. 12.00 - 17.00 but since there is no electric light the cottage closes at dusk if earlier than 17.00. The cottage is occasionally closed due to military manoeuvres.

Continue past the viewing area for ¼ mile and just before the main road, is Clouds Hill cottage on the right.

MORETON

The village of Moreton passed into the Frampton family by marriage in the fourteenth century. The Framptons were cousins of T. E. Lawrence. It was James Frampton, High Sheriff of Dorset, who framed and arrested the Tolpuddle Martyrs under a trumped up charge of taking an illegal oath.

T. E. Lawrence died in 1935 at the age of 46. It had been planned that he should be buried in St Paul's Cathedral. However due to the political situation at the time, this was not possible and it was decided that he should be buried in the church of St Nicholas in the small village of Moreton. The funeral was attended by Winston and Mrs Churchill, as well as Bernard Shaw. The church is reached by going through the white 'Dorset Gate' of Moreton House and walking down the drive for about 50 yards. The church is on the right. There have been three churches on the site. The first, much smaller than the present one, was built around 1190. It was rebuilt in 1410 and again in 1776. It was struck by a bomb in 1940 during the Second World War and was not refurbished until 1950. At the time the original stained glass windows were not replaced. Since then they have been replaced by a series of engraved glass windows, created and signed by Sir Laurence Whistler. The windows, which were created over a period of 30 years, are world famous and St Nicholas' church is the only one in England where every window has been designed by the same person and probably the only church in the world where all the windows are engraved glass. Prior to 1776 there was a peal of five bells but this was reduced to two bells in the new church because the Framptons complained that the ringers drank too much whilst ringing. (At the time it was normal to pay ringers with beer.) The church must be one of the most beautiful small churches in England.

Church of St Nicholas, Moreton, Dorset DT2 8RG.

Scenes of the occasion of Lawrence's funeral can be seen in the Lawrence Room at the Tea Room. The estate bier that carried the coffin is there, as also are some of the many correspondences between Lawrence and the Frampton family from whom he purchased Clouds Hill. There is a small collection of glass in the display cabinet that belonged to Roger Coker, rector of the church from 1775 to 1813. The Tea Room used to be the local school and the school provided the choir at Lawrence's funeral.

Moreton Tea Rooms

The Moreton Tea Rooms, Moreton, Dorset DT2 8RG. Tel: 01929 463 647. Open: Daily from March to October 10.00 - 17.00 and from November to December on Wednesday - Sunday from 10.00 - 16.00.

An excellent free leaflet entitled *Lawrence of Arabia Walking Trail* is available from the Wareham Information Centre and gives details of his life in the area.

Lawrence's grave is at the far end of the churchyard, beneath the cypress tree

The churchyard containing Lawrence's grave is separate from the church and can be reached through the portico

Leave Clouds Hill Cottage and turn right. 100 yards further on, turn left. 1½ miles further on turn left on to the B3390 Weymouth Road. Just over ½ mile further on turn left into Hurst Road. 1 mile further on, fork left and the village of Moreton is 100 yards away To return to the roundabout near Monkey World, continue past the churchyard for 3½ miles. Turn left and the roundabout is ½ mile further on.

TOLPUDDLE

The small village of Tolpuddle, 12 miles west of Poole, is one of the most famous villages in the world. The village existed at the time of the Domesday Book and derives its name from the fact that originally it belonged to Tola, a servant of King Cnut, and is on the River Piddle (or the River Trent as it is more commonly called). It was here, under a giant sycamore tree, that a group of six men, later to be known as the Tolpuddle Martyrs, used to meet. The six men were James Brine, James Hammett, George and James Loveless and Thomas and John Standfield. Men working around them were being paid ten shillings per week but, despite promises from their employer to pay them the same amount, they were only paid nine shillings. This was later reduced to eight shillings per week and then seven shillings. When they were told that this was to be reduced still further to six shillings they formed the Friendly Society of Agricultural Labourers (FSAL) to try to improve their conditions. This was effectively the first trade union. Membership of FSAL cost one shilling and they swore an oath of loyalty that they would never tell anyone the secrets of the society. Although trade unions had effectively been declared legal in 1824, the men were arrested on 24 February 1834 and charged under the 1797 Mutiny Act (intended to stop naval mutinies) and found guilty of taking an illegal oath. Under pressure from the Whig government of Lord Melbourne, which was bitterly opposed to any trade union movement that would challenge the interest of landowners, the men were hurriedly deported to the penal colonies of New South Wales for hard labour for a period of seven years. Such was the outcry at the sentence, the first mass trade union protest took place with 250,000 people signing a petition and 30,000 people marching on Whitehall. After fierce parliamentary debate, the sentences were remitted. Four of the six were released in 1836 and returned to England before moving to Canada. Only James Hammet, who was

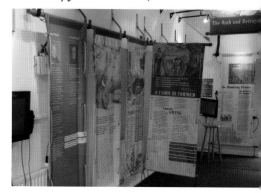

released a year later, returned and settled in Tolpuddle. He died in 1891 and is buried in the churchyard. Each summer on the third weekend in July, a commemoration to the Martyrs takes palace in the village, with speakers coming from trades unions from all over the world.

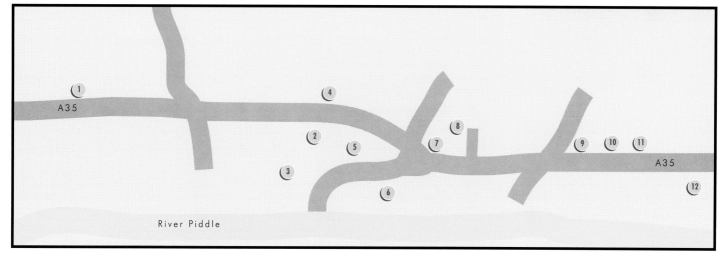

1. In 1934 to commemorate the centenary of the trial of the Martyrs, the Trades Union Congress built six memorial cottages, one dedicated to each of the Martyrs, to house agricultural workers, together with a museum. In front of the cottages is a sculpture of George Loveless waiting to be transported at the start of his journey to Australia.

2. The parish church of St John the Evangelist is constructed of flint and stone, with part of it dating from the twelfth century. The grave of James Hammett is in the north-west corner of the churchyard and is clearly signposted.

3. From the south of the church can be seen the listed Manor House dating from the seventeenth century. Originally it was a home for the local monks.

4. Opposite the church are the Grade II listed Church Hill Cottages dating from the late eighteenth century.

5. The Martyrs' Tree is the largest sycamore tree in Dorset. It is believed to date from the 1680s, long before the Martyrs met under it in 1834. It is designated one of the 50 Great British Trees in recognition of its place in the national heritage. Close by the tree on the village green is a commemorative seat and shelter erected in 1934.

6. Opposite the village green is a group of three listed sixteenth century cottages.

7. The Village Hall opposite the cottages was built in 1857 and was originally the local school.

8. Tolpuddle Hall is reached by walking up a short driveway. Parts of the hall date from the sixteenth century and was originally the village vicarage. It is now a farmhouse but is currently unoccupied.

9. The Martyrs Inn stands on the site of the former Crown Inn which was one of three original inns in the village before it was destroyed by fire in the early part of the twentieth century.

10. Standfield's Cottage, also known as Martyrs Cottage, was built in the eighteenth century. It was here, in Thomas Standfield's home, that the Martys met before they were betrayed.

11. Next to Standfield's Cottage is the original Methodist chapel, built in 1818, where the Martyrs worshipped.

12. Further along the road on the right is the current chapel built in 1861. At its entrance is a memorial arch to the Martyrs which was added in 1912.

Tolpuddle Martyrs Museum, Tolpuddle, Dorchester, Dorset DT2 7EH. Tel: 01305 848237. Open: April to October, Tuesday - Saturday 10.00 - 17.00, Sunday 11.00 - 17.00, Closed Mondays. November to March: Thursday - Saturday 10.00 - 16.00, Sunday 11.00 - 16.00, Closed Monday - Wednesday.

Leave Moreton the way you came with the Tea Room on the right. After 100 yards fork right. At the junction ¾ mile ahead, turn right onto the B3390. After 2¼ miles, just after the Affpuddle sign, turn left signposted Tolpuddle. At the junction 1½ miles later turn left; the museum is 200 yards on the right.

From Bournemouth, take the Wessex Way and join the A35 to Poole and later Dorchester. About 20 miles from Bournemouth the road to Tolpuddle is clearly signposted on the left. The museum is at the far end of the village, about 1 mile after leaving the A35.

AFFPUDDLE

When the monasteries were dissolved by Henry VIII, Sir Oliver Laurence bought Affpuddle, including the church. It is likely for this reason that the church is dedicated to his namesake St Laurence, patron saint of comedians, butchers and roasters. (The saint is said to have been martyred by being roasted on a spit and during the process had asked to be turned over because one side of him was not properly cooked.) Part of the church dates from the early thirteenth century although it has been rebuilt and repaired a number of times since. The carved pew ends and pulpit are what the church is rightly famous for and some of the carvings date back to 1547. The Norman font dates from the twelfth century.

In the church's grounds is the Peace Garden with a shrine dedicated to those who gave their lives in World War II. It was given to the church by Sir Ernest Debenham, whose family founded the Debenham Stores and who purchased a large part of the estate from the Frampton family in 1914. Gravestones to various members of the Debenham family are in evidence.

Opposite the shrine and on the opposite side of the River Piddle (also known as the Trent or Puddle), is what was the village's old mill. Affpuddle has won the award of Best Kept Hamlet for the last three years.

Leave Tolpuddle by the road (The Green) in front of the Martyr's Tree. After ¼ mile bear left and a mile further on is the church of St Laurence.

BRIANTSPUDDLE

Briantspuddle must rank as one of the prettiest villages in Dorset. On the outskirts is the village's War Memorial to commemorate those who lost their lives in the First World War. It was dedicated one day after the signing of the Armistice in August 1918. Close by is the attractive Old Post. The gravel road from the memorial leads to Bladen Valley with a number of thatched cottages that were built for the farm workers.

Continuing past the memorial leads to the centre of the village with its beautiful thatched cottages. It was in Briantspuddle that Sir Ernest Debenham carried out an agriculture experiment and successfully built his model farm, in which residents produced their own food and lived off the land. He would not permit any pub to be built in the village and it was left to his brother to later start a social club. The houses are numbered in the order that the rent was collected.

The village hall is a converted 200 year old barn and next to it is the village's only shop, which also houses the post office. The shop used to be a granary and during its time has housed farm-workers and acted as a youth club. The post office and shop are run by volunteers and are only open for two or three hours every morning. The shop sells a few souvenirs. Its entrance is at the rear.

200 yards past the village hall is the Old Dairy known as the 'Ring' by the locals which was where the farm vehicles used to load. Walking up the road beside the Ring you can see many of the buildings that made up the Old Dairy, including the Granary, and which have now been converted into residential accommodation. Opposite the Ring is one of the original 12 cottages and the oldest building in the village dating back to the early seventeenth century.

BERE REGIS

beautiful carved ends date from the sixteenth century. The beauty of the stained glass windows and of the tiling on the floor matches the overall beauty of the church.

On the opposite side of Elder Road are watercress fields alongside the Bere Stream. As you leave Elder Road more of the fields can be seen ahead of you and the entrance to them is along the road to the right.

St John the Baptist church in Bere Regis was built around 1050 and has been added to and modified over the centuries so the church today contains architecture from the eleventh to sixteenth centuries. It is likely that King John was a regular visitor here. Prior to 1050 it is thought that there was a timber church on the site. At one time it was the most richly endowed church belonging to Salisbury Cathedral. The two central columns on the south side with carvings at the corners

of the capitals date from the twelfth century. The magnificent carved ceiling of the nave, unique for Dorset, dates from 1485 and is believed to have been a gift from Cardinal Morton. The 12 carved figures represent the apostles. A coin in the electric slot-meter illuminates the ceiling and allows visitors to see it in all its beauty. The pews with their

Bere Regis St John The Baptist church, Bere Regis, BH20 7HQ. Tel: 01929 471262. Open daily but guided tours from May to September on Tuesdays starting at 11.00 and Thursdays starting at 15.00.

From Briantspuddle, continue past the Ring which bears right through the tiny hamlet of Throop. After 1 mile turn left at the junction. 1 mile further on is the turning to Turnerspuddle with its now almost defunct church but which is still occasionally used for funeral services. Continue past this turning for another ½ mile to the next road junction where you again turn left. ¾ mile further on the left is Elder Road in which you can park and from which a path leads to the church.

St John the Baptist, Bere Regis

SHITTERTON

Shitterton has the distinction of having one of the top ten rudest place names in the country. Although those living in the hamlet seem to be proud of its name, or at the very least not ashamed of it, those in neighbouring Bere Regis prefer to pronounce it as 'Sitterton'. The hamlet is delightful and must be one of the prettiest in Dorset. It consists of a farm and a number of beautiful thatched cottages, one of which is appropriately named 'Pooh Corner'.

The name of the hamlet derives from the sewage channel that used to flow through the village along what is now the Bere Stream. The stream is now crystal clear and feeds the watercress fields in Bere Regis. For many years there was no sign indicating the name of the hamlet since each time a sign was erected it was stolen. However the locals were asked by the council to contribute to have a stone sign and one was erected in 2010.

FARMER PALMER'S FARM PARK

The park is designed specifically for children up to 8 years of age. The attraction has won several awards. Much of the farm is undercover so it is not particularly weather dependent. There is a full series of events throughout the day, which permit children to hold and touch the animals.

Farmer Palmer's Farm Park, Wareham Road, Organford, Poole, BH16 6EU Tel: 01202 622022 Open: All year 10.00 - 16.00 (1730 in summer).

From Bere Regis church, turn left on leaving Elder Road and continue ¼ mile to the roundabout. Turn right on to the A35 to Bournemouth. 7 miles further on is the turning to Farmer Palmer's.

Turn left on leaving Elder Road and then left again through Bere Regis. The entrance to the hamlet is ⅓ mile on the left.

COURTYARD CENTRE

The centre was originally a farm built in the early eighteenth century. The three large oak trees at the entrance were planted in 1720 when the large barn was built. The present owners purchased the site in 1985 when it was practically derelict. Today the centre houses a number of art and craft units where visitors can purchase articles or learn the crafts by a series of lessons. There is a licensed restaurant

The Courtyard Craft Centre, Huntick Road, Lytchett Minster, Poole, Dorset BH16 6BA Tel: 01202 631030. Open: Daily, although some stalls are closed on Mondays.

From the turning to Farmer Palmer's, continue along the A35 for ¾ mile to the roundabout. Turn left. The centre is then clearly signposted.

WIMBORNE MINSTER

The town of Wimborne Minster lies between the Rivers Stour and Allen, the latter splitting up as it passes through the town. Julian's Bridge, which crosses the River Stour on the east of the town, was built in 1636 to replace an earlier bridge and was subsequently widened in 1844. It was built with niches along its length to allow pedestrians to move out of the road when coaches passed. These niches are still needed as there are no pavements. Wimborne Minster claims that it has the largest markets in the south of England and they are held every Friday (including the weekly Farmers' Market), Saturday (including the Giant Car Boot market) and Sunday. (For further details phone 01202 841212). The marketplace is reached by going east along East Street, crossing over the roundabout at Lewens Lane and into Leigh Road. It is a few hundred yards further along on the right. According to the Office for National Statistics, people in Wimborne Minster live longer than anywhere else in the UK. There is a debate on the actual name of the town. The Ordnance Survey map calls it 'Wimborne Minster', as do most of the locals, whereas the Post Office insists it is simply 'Wimborne'.

WIMBORNE MINSTER TOWN TRAIL

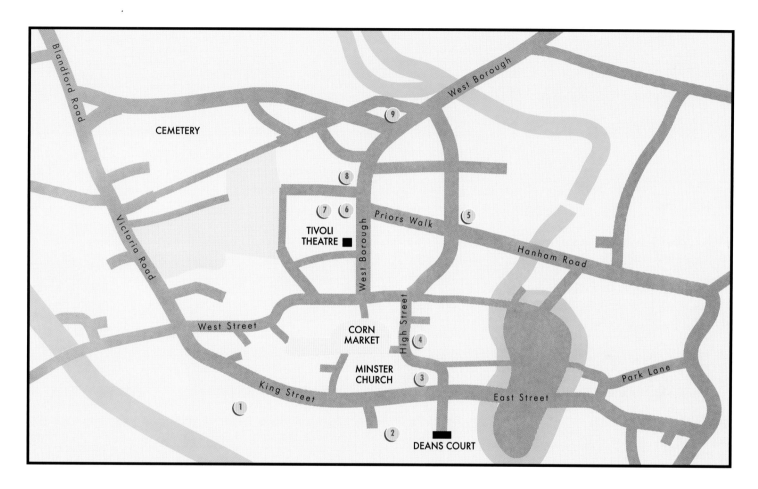

1. The trail starts at the **Wimborne Minster Model Town**. The model is a one-tenth scale reconstruction of Wimborne Minster as it was in the early 1950s. The idea for the scale model began in the 1940s when photos of the town were taken. A site was found and the scale of 1:10 decided upon as this would permit most of the town centre to be constructed in the space available. Construction of the buildings in concrete, with beech window frames, started in the late 1940s and the site opened to the public for the first time in 1951.

The site changed ownership several times and was finally purchased by a developer who closed the attraction, which subsequently fell into disrepair. In the late 1980s the models were given to the town and they were re-erected on the existing site, which re-opened to the public in 1991. In the meantime the shops were provided with model goods for display in the widows and in particular the interior of the church was recreated.

Wimborne Minster Model Town & Gardens, King Street, Wimborne BH21 1DY Tel: 01202 881924. Open: March to November, 10.00 - 17.00.

Follow the directions to Stapehill Abbey (see page 49) and continue on for ½ mile. Take the second exit at the round-about onto the A31. After 2 miles turn right at the round-about (3rd exit). After 1¼ miles turn right on the B3078. After 1 mile cross the mini roundabout and follow the road round. The Model Town is on the left.

2. Going east along King Street and the first turning on the right leads to the beautiful **Old Grammar School** built in 1851 but converted into flats in the 1980s. Continuing with the church on your left, on the right is Deans Court Lane leading to Deans Court, whose gardens cover an area of 13 acres alongside the River Allen and include specimen trees, lawns and borders. Originally the house

was the church's Deanery. The kitchen garden has a long serpentine wall, built during the 1790s by prisoners from the Napoleonic Wars. The house has been in the same family since 1548.

Deans Court, Deans Court Lane, East Street, Wimborne, Dorset BH21 1EE . The gardens are open on selected days from April to September. Tel: 01202 886116 or 01202 880515 Tours by written agreement.

3. Turning left along High Street and round the bend on the left is the grey stone building of **Church House** built in 1906; it used to be the main meeting and function room for the Wimborne Minster church.

4. Continuing along the High Street and again passing Wimborne Minster church, you come to the Tourist Information Centre withthe **Priest's House Museum** on the right. The museum is in a 10 room, sixteenth century Grade II* listed town house which has been

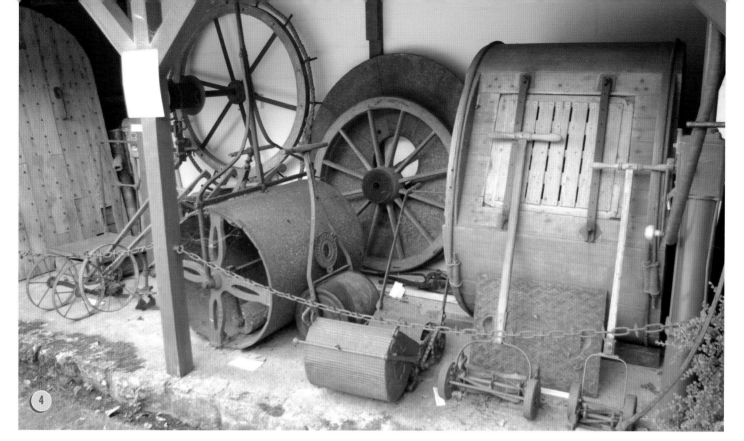

④

restored to show, by means of a number of period rooms, how it was to live and work in various periods in the past. The building used to be the home of past ministers of the church opposite and there are exhibits relating to this.

There is a seventeenth century hall, an 18th century Georgian parlour and a Victorian kitchen and stationery shop. The latter was next door to the current building and its contents were closed to the outside world for 30 years; these are now used in the reconstruction. Also recreated is the ironmonger's that operated from the building from 1872 to 1960, again using stock from the original shop. The East Dorset Villages Gallery depicts community life as it was in terms of shopping, school and church. The archaeological display gives the story of the area from prehistoric times up to the modern day and contains a wealth of material relating to the history of the area. It is one of the smallest museums in the country to have gained the Sandford Award for Excellence in Heritage Education, which it has now won four times. A delightful walled garden stretches down to the banks of the River Allen and the 1920s Boathouse is now a tea room where light refreshments can be bought.

Next to the museum is the Albion Inn built in the seventeenth century and which is the oldest licensed house remaining in the town. The coaching arch would have led to stabling and the coach carrying the *Tolpuddle Martyrs* is believed to have stopped here on the way to the convict ship that carried the men to Australia. Unfortunately the inn was severely damaged by fire in July 2009 along with neighbouring shops. Fortunately the museum was saved.

The Priest's House Museum and Garden, 23-27 High Street, Wimborne Minster, Dorset BH21 1HR. Tel: 01202 882533 Open: April to October, Monday - Saturday 10.30 - 16.30.

5. Continuing along High Street you reach the Square, soon to be regenerated. Go right at the Square into East Borough. The last house

on the left before coming to the crossroad is East Borough Cottage built in 1640. Matthew Prior, Diplomat and Poet, was born here in 1664. On the opposite side of the road in Hanham Road is **Allendale House** built in 1823 for the Castleman family. It is now the home of the East Dorset Heritage Trust.

6. Walking west along Priors Walk into West Borough and directly opposite is the **Town Hall**.

7. Behind the Town Hall is the **Jubilee Garden** which was planted to celebrate Queen Elizabeth II's Golden Jubilee. It is in the style of a seventeenth century Physicke Garden in that only plants in existence in the seventeenth century and used for either medicinal or culinary purposes or for dyeing clothes are included. The gazebo is now the headquarters of the Wimborne Civic Society.

8. Just to the north of the Town Hall is **Gulliver House**, which was the home of Wimborne's most famous smuggler Isaac Gulliver, (page 143).

9. Several hundred yards further to the north is **Walford Mill**. The existing mill is thought to have been built during the 1760s although there is evidence that there was a mill on the site in the sixteenth century. The name 'Walford' is an old English word for 'uncertain' and refers to the uncertainty in crossing the river at this point – the Mill is on an island formed by the River Allen, the Mill Stream and

the Mill Pond. Milling continued here until 1966, after which the mill was used for a variety of purposes. On the death of its owner Mr Bankes in 1982, it passed into the hands of the National Trust who in turn sold it to East Dorset District Council in 1983, together with 13 acres of surrounding land. The mill is now an exhibition and craft centre, with a strong educational purpose. There are three workshops where local craftspeople can be seen working at such crafts as silk weaving, jewellery making and creating stained glass. They will also produce items to order. Planning permission was granted in April 2009 for a £3m development that will replace the existing restaurant with additional education and exhibition space and to form a new entrance from a bridge over the River Allen.

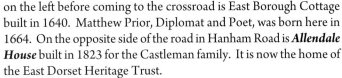

Walford Mill Crafts, Stone Lane, Wimborne, Dorset BH21 1NL. Tel: 01202 841400. Open: Monday - Saturday 10.00 - 17.00; Sunday 12.00 - 17.00. Closed Mondays from January to March. Free admission. Licensed restaurant.

Going south along West Borough you come to the **Tivoli Theatre** built in the eighteenth century. It closed in 1980 but re-opened ten years later and now offers several forms of entertainment (Tel: 01202 885566). Continuing south brings you back to **Wimborne Minster church.**

A more detailed Town Trail can be obtained for £1 from the Wimborne Tourist Information Centre.

WIMBORNE MINSTER CHURCH

The church is on a site where, in 705, there was a nunnery and abbey established by Saint Cuthburga, sister of King Ina, King of the West Saxons. Later a monastery was built alongside the abbey. In 1013 the Danes invaded the area and destroyed the nunnery (which was never rebuilt), but the abbey and monastery survived. The Normans repaired and enlarged the building between 1120 and 1180. There have been additions to the church since, notably in the thirteenth and fourteenth centuries; the last addition being the vestry which was added at the end of the nineteenth century. However most of the building is Norman, although parts, notably the central tower and nave, date from the Saxon era.

There are several points of interest:

Alfred the Great buried his brother, King Ethelred, in the church in 871. The exact location of the grave is not known but is thought to be in one of the walls. A brass plaque dedicated to the King is next to the altar and another stating that it is the only such plaque dedicated to an English King.

On the first floor is a chained library with more than 400 books, half of which are over 300 years old, with the earliest dated 1343. It is one of only four surviving chained libraries in the world and the second largest in the country. It was formed in 1686 and became

other reason given is that Sir Edmund was a Catholic who were known as 'left footers', hence the two left feet.

The clock in the Baptistry is based on the pre-Copernican system of astronomy when it was believed that the sun travelled round the earth. Most of the workings of the clock date from the fourteenth century, although the face and dial are significantly older.

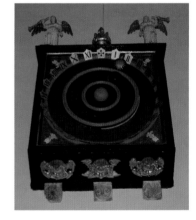

High up on the west tower is the church's Quarter Jack, a Grenadier, that strikes two bells every quarter of an hour. It dates from 1612.

Other points of interest in the church are the Beaufort tomb where the grandson of John of Gaunt is depicted as holding hands with his wife, the murals which date from the thirteenth - fifteenth centuries and the Saxon chest that is believed to have held religious relics.

Wimborne Minster Church, High Street, Wimborne Minster, BH21 1HT.

chained when opened to the public in the latter part of the seventeenth century. When studying the books readers usually stood up. It is likely that the fixed desk was installed in the nineteenth century.

The organ has over 3,000 pipes, the oldest of which dates from 1664. The orchestral trumpets were installed in 1965 when the organ was overhauled.

Anthony Ettrick was Recorder and Magistrate of Poole. He was convinced that he would die in 1693 and had his coffin inscribed as such. However he died 10 years later and the date on his coffin had to be changed. He also stipulated that he should not be buried 'within the church or without it - neither below the ground nor above it'. To satisfy this stipulation, his coffin was place in a recess in the church's wall.

The monument to Sir Edmund Uvedale appears to have two left feet. Two possible explanations for this are given by the guides. One is that when the right foot had to be repaired, the craftsman was given Sir Edmund's left foot to aid him and a straight copy was made. The

GREEN MEN

The Green Man is represented in sculpture, usually in wood or stone, by a face surrounded with leaves; they can also appear in books, metalwork and stained glass. Frequently the leaves may be on branches emanating from the nose, mouth or other parts of the face. Almost invariably the face is male, although occasionally the face is that of a woman. The sculptures are sometimes hidden from view. They are pagan in origin and are believed to have a fertility connection and to be a sign of rebirth. They appear in many countries and first appeared in England in the twelfth century, although they were not given their name 'Green Man' until the late 1930s. Most Green Men appear to be friendly but some have demon-like features. Many appear in medieval churches. The Green Man in Wimborne Minster is carved under the misericord next to the Rector's stool and is normally hidden from view. Visitors will need to ask the guides if they wish to see it.

There is a Green Man on each of the four corners of the chapel building in Bournemouth's Wimborne Road Cemetery, all slightly different but all with leaves sprouting from their mouths.

The Earthlights Tea Room in Swanage has seven Green Men and one Green Woman above the arches.

'Green Man' as a pub name appears to date from the seventeenth century. Some pubs changed their signs from a traditional Green Man to that of a Robin Hood type person. The O'Neill pub on Old Christchurch Road near the Lansdowne Road in Bournemouth has a very distinct Green Woman.

Above: Wimborne Minister

Left: Wimborne Road Cemetery

Earthlights Tea Room

O'Neill pub

KINGSTON LACY HOUSE

Sir John Bankes, who resided at Corfe Castle, supported King Charles I during the Civil War. When the castle fell to the Parliamentarians and was demolished, the Bankes family looked for a site on the 8,000 acres of land they owned on which to build a new house. They settled on the site near to Wimborne Minster. The house took two years to build and was completed in 1665; it replaced a medieval manor that had been destroyed in the Civil War. Substantial work was carried out on the house in the late nineteenth century when the building was re-faced in stone and four tall chimneys were added. The house remained in the Bankes family until 1981 when on the death of Henry Bankes it was bequeathed along with Corfe Castle, Walford Mill and other estates he owned to the National Trust. At the time it was the largest donation ever made to the Trust.

The Grade I listed building contains an outstanding collection of paintings dating back over 400 years, including works by Reubens, Van Dyck, Titian, Breughel, Reynolds, Murillo and

The stables have been converted into a restaurant and café.

Velazquez. William Bankes travelled extensively in the late nineteenth century and brought many treasures back to Kingston Lacy. Of particular note is the spectacular marble staircase and the Spanish Room, whose walls are hung with gilded leather. In the library are the large keys of the destroyed Corfe Castle. He acquired the largest collection of Egyptian antiquities in the world, including the large obelisk which stands in the grounds, as well as other marble statues.

The kitchen gardens, which date back to 1874, fell into decline during the Second World War and only now are they being returned to their former beauty. Some of the original glass houses have survived and will be used to grow produce for use in the restaurant or for sale to the public. A group of saddleback pigs is being used to help clear the gardens, while at the same time fertilise them.

Kingston Lacy House, Park & Garden, Wimborne Minster, BH21 4EA Tel: 01202 883402 (Monday-Friday) 01202 842913 (Saturday and Sunday). Open: The house is open from March to November, Wednesday-Sunday 11.00 - 16.00. The gardens, park, shop and stables restaurant are open all year, other than from late December to early February. Due to the large number of visitors, admission may be by timed ticket on bank holiday weekends.

Leave Wimborne on the B3082. The road passes in front of the Town Hall and then turns left. The entrance to Kingston Lacy House is 2 miles along on the left.

BADBURY RINGS

the entrance are three barrows (ancient grave mounds) indicating that this was a traditional place of burial.

There are good views from the top of the fort, including of the two mile long Beech Avenue (B3082) with its beech trees that lead from Kingston Lacy to the Rings. The trees were planted in 1835 as a gift from William Bankes to his mother Frances, with 365 trees down one side of the road and 366 down the other. The National Trust is doing all it can to prolong their life but have planted a second row of hornbeam trees as a replacement for the time when the original trees have to be felled.

Open: There is ample car parking space which is open from 09.00 - 16.00 during the winter and 09.00 - 20.00 in the summer. Free admittance. Dogs are not allowed into the Rings.

Follow the directions to Kingston Lacy and continue for another 1½ miles. The track leading to Badbury Rings is on the right and the car park ¼ mile further on.

This Iron Age hill fort has never been excavated. It dates from around 800 BC and is part of the Kingston Lacy estate. Legend has it that this is the site where King Arthur had his victory over the Saxon King Cedric in the fifth century and then after his death he turned himself into a raven so as to live within the wood that is nearby. Indeed it is likely that the woods were used for breeding ravens.

The Neolithic fort consists of three concentric rings of banks and ditches which surround the seven hectare fort which is now filled with pine trees. As the ditches were dug the soil that was removed would have been piled on the inner side to form the ramparts. The ditches are now about 20 foot deep (and the ramparts another 20 foot high). They would have been significantly deeper at the time they were built but over the years the soil forming the ramparts has fallen back into them. The fort itself would have been surrounded by a timber battlement to give protection to the defenders. There are circular depressions in the ground about 10 foot in diameter that almost certainly were made by houses at the time. In total the fort is 330 foot high. There were two entrances, one to the east and the other to the west, both of which were staggered to make attack more difficult and would have had large wooden gates. It would have been almost impossible to conquer the fort at the time it was built as the simple shoes worn by an Iron-Age warrior would not have allowed enough support to climb the loose surface of the ramparts. However the fort's slippery slopes would not have caused any problem to the Romans under Emperor Claudius when they arrived in the area. At

WHITEMILL AND ITS THREE PARISHES

St Bartholomew's church, Shapwick, is one of three churches near Whitemill. Parts of the church date from the eleventh century, although most of it dates from the fourteenth century. A major refurbishment took place in 1880. The church has five bells which until recently had not been usable for 30 years. The newest was consecrated in August 2009 whilst one of the others is said to be the oldest bell in Dorset and has Old English writing engraved on it To view the bells contact the Verger and Tower Keeper, John Whelan (Tel: 01258 858268 or 01258 857255). The steps to the bells are steep and narrow. The graveyard has many old headstones covered with lichens indicating their age. (Lichens are a mixture of algae and fungi and are slow growing but can live for thousands of years.) From the car park at the side of the church is a style leading to the Stour River. The river floods most years and there are metal barriers at the church entrance to try to prevent the flood waters reaching the church.

Leaving Bradbury Rings, the road directly opposite leads to Shapwick, which is 1½ miles further on. The church is 200 yards along the road opposite the main road.

Whitemill was built in 1776 although it is likely that there was at least one, if not two, mills on the site as far back as the twelfth century. This, or any earlier mills, are likely to have been of wooden construction. To increase the flow of the river to the mill a series of weirs were built up river. During floods the ground floor of the mill is often covered with water and a severe flood destroyed some of the working parts of the mill in 1866 so that it could no longer work by water power. Part of the mill was then converted so as to run from a portable steam engine but a few years later all milling stopped. For the next 85 years the mill was used as a shed. The mill is part of the Kingston Lacy estate and passed into the hands of the National Trust in 1982 and 12 years later work commenced on the property to save it for the Nation. It is now the home of the custodian and, as the National Trust points out, one of the few properties in the Trust's care that has a resident custodian. The reason it is called 'Whitemill' is not known but the Romans, after destroying the hillfort of **Badbury Rings**, built a town close by which they called 'Vindocladia' - 'the Place of White Walls' and this may be the reason for the mill's name.

Whitemill, Open: Saturdays, Sundays and Bank Holiday Mondays between Easter and October.

On leaving Chuch Road in Shapwick, turn right and the mill is 1½ miles on the right.

The **Whitemill Bridge** with its eight decorative arches crosses the River Stour and dates from around the sixteenth century, although

the timber pilings on which it stands date from the twelfth century. This is thought to be the oldest bridge site in Dorset. The bridge is the meeting point of three parishes, namely Shapwick, Pamphill and Sturminster Marshall; each has its own interesting church.

Whitemill Bridge is just beyond Whitemill. The best view is from the field on the opposite side of the road to the mill.

St Mary The Virgin church in Sturminster Marshal was the site of a Norman stone church in the twelfth century, which was extended over the next two centuries. The tower fell down in 1802 and was rebuilt three years later. Three of the church's peel of six bells date from 1350 and are said to be among the oldest bells in Dorset.

St Stephen's church in Pamphill is usually referred to as St Stephen's, Kingston Lacy. The Bankes family paid for it to be built but then bequeathed it to the village of Pamphill in the 1920s and hence it was not bequeathed to the National Trust in 1982 with the rest of the Bankes' estate. The original church was built near the beginning of the thirteenth century but was destroyed in the sixteenth century and was not replaced until the present church was built in 1906. It is built of Studland sandstone and Purbeck stone which gives it its unique appearance. The Bankes family had a private entrance on the north side so they could walk directly in from their estate.

Sturminster is a further 5 miles beyond Whitemill.

The road leading to the church is lined with oak trees

Leaving the Whitemill car park, turn left (signpost at the start of the road says Cowgrove and Wimborne). After 2½ miles turn left and then after 200 yards left again. The drive leading to the church is ¼ mile at the end of the road.

SMUGGLERS

Smuggling was rife everywhere in the eighteenth and nineteenth centuries, no more so than in East Dorset. It had been going on for centuries in a small way but during the Civil War a tax was placed on essential commodities. As the war continued and then followed by more wars with Europe, taxes were increased in a desperate attempt to raise money to pay for them. The price of tea consisted of 70% tax and so more and more people bought smuggled tea. By the end of the eighteenth century it was estimated that nine out of ten families were involved in some way with smuggling. Heavy punishments were introduce but this made little difference due to the lack of law enforcement. Smuggling was a way of life for many, especially the poor.

One of the most famous gangs, said to number in excess of 500 members, was the ruthless and blood-thirsty Hawkhurst Gang, headed by Thomas Kingsmill, based in Hawkhurst, Sussex. In September 1747 the gang was waiting on the Sussex shore for the arrival of a cutter *The Three Brothers* carrying a cargo of brandy, rum and tea. The cutter was intercepted by the customs cutter *Swift* off the coast of Dorset. After a six hour chase, the gang surrendered and the *Swift* escorted *The Three Brothers* into Poole Harbour and the contraband was off-loaded into the Customs House on Poole Quay.

Poole Customs House

On 7 October 1747 The Hawkhurst Gang raided the Customs House and retrieved their captured contraband. They returned triumphantly to Hawkhurst. However a large reward was posted for information leading to their capture and one of the gang by the name of Chater turned informant. Subsequently he and a customs officer were captured by the gang. Chater was brutally beaten, mutilated, thrown down a well and then stones dropped on him. The customs officer met with a similar fate, other than he was buried alive. Members of the gang were subsequently hunted down and several of them hanged.

Not all smuggling gangs were so violent. The most famous smuggler of the time was Isaac Gulliver, born in 1745, who claimed that he had never hurt anyone. Indeed he had a Robin Hood type reputation. He had a private army, a fleet of 15 ships, a string of properties and a network of tunnels by which he was able to move his contraband about. He paid the poor more for one night's work then they could otherwise earn in a week. He frequently unloaded his contraband during the day, not worrying about the customs officers. It was also common for more than one ship to be unloading its contraband at the same time and to have a two mile convoy of horses and carts transporting his contraband inland. He eventually applied for and was granted the King's pardon in 1782. He settled in Wimborne Minster in Gulliver House and was buried in Wimborne Minster church where there is a plaque to his memory on the wall to the right near the entrance.

There was a pitched battle at Mudeford on 14 July 1784 when two Revenue cutters discovered a gang of smugglers on the beach. There were literally tons of tea and over 100,000 gallons of brandy on the shore with hundreds of horses and carts removing the contraband. A Revenue ship's captain tried to capture the smugglers but when the Revenue men attempted to go ashore they were met by a hail of musket fire. The smugglers' boats were captured but the contraband and smugglers disappeared into the night.

Gulliver House

Kinson Church

There was also a pitched battle in 1787 around what is now the location of Bournemouth Pier. The smugglers were spotted unloading their contraband and were driven off by armed Revenue men. However the gang soon returned with other members who were now fully armed. They drove off the Revenue men and recaptured their goods which were taken up the Chine (now the Lower, Central and Upper Gardens) to Coy Pond for allocating to the waiting people.

The Isle of Purbeck was perfect for smuggling with many coves along the coast, a gently sloping beach and sand for hiding the barrels of liquor if necessary. One of the places where the contraband was stored was the church in Langton Matravers, allegedly without the knowledge of the vicar. Apparently a large shipment of brandy, around 200 kegs, was stored in the roof of the church. The weight was too much and the ceiling fell down during a Sunday service killing one of the congregation and seriously injuring many of the others. The village was the headquarters for the smuggling in the area.

Lewis Tregonwell is generally regarded as the founder of Bournemouth. He had a servant by the name of Symes for whom he built a home. When this building was demolished they found underneath it a secret chamber. The Symes family were known to be smugglers and the question has to be asked whether Tregonwell himself was involved in smuggling.

Kinson in Bournemouth was the centre of a smuggling ring with a network of tunnels beneath the church of St Andrew. Many of the early graves in the graveyard are those of smugglers, the most famous being that of Robert Trotman who was killed on the beach near Bournemouth in 1765, whilst smuggling tea.

The grave in front of Kinson church was said to be a dummy grave in which smugglers stored their contraband. However the carving on the grave stone states that it contains the bodies of William Oakley and his wife Jane and records show that there was a William Oakley living in the parish at that time.

The golden age of smuggling came to an end during the nineteenth century when the punitive taxes, the evasion of which made smuggling so profitable and indeed almost essential for the ordinary person to live, were reduced.

For those who want to follow a smugglers trail walk lasting around 2½ - 3 hours, then the National Trust issue leaflet a leaflet called *Smugglers' Ways* taking in the areas of Worth Matravers, Winspit & Seacombe.

For further information on smuggling read *Smugglers' Dorset* by Robert Westwood.